Title and Copyright

The Serger and Overlock Master Guide

Copyright © 2014 by Clifford L Blodget

Paperback Edition ISBN 978-0-9900227-5-6

Published 2014 by Blodget Publishing, LLC.

blodgetpublishing@gmail.com

Dedication

This book is dedicated to my wife and family.

Table of Contents

Introduction

About this book - This is the most comprehensive and up to date book about sergers available covering all skill levels from basic to expert. Although advanced topics are covered the book is easy to navigate and understand. Many people find threading a serger to be difficult, so an entire chapter is dedicated to threading and basic use. The book goes on to cover advanced topics such as troubleshooting, adjustment, maintenance & repair. Covered in-depth are adjusting tension, stitches, decorative stitches, needles, feet, thread and more.

From home sergers to industrial overlock machines and coverstitch machines many of the latest machines are featured with insights on features, capabilities and best use for each model or class of machine. Buying a serger can be frustrating and time consuming because of the overwhelming number of features and types of machines that are available. The buying recommendations will help you cut through the confusion and figure out what features you really need.

Most people have a love/hate relationship with their serger. Everything is great when the machine is working good but most people hate them when frustrating problems arise. This book will empower you to eliminate the hate part of the relationship and put you in control of the machine. In depth sections on adjusting tension and troubleshooting will help you handle most problems (and know which problems not to tackle). Above all sergers are creative tools. If you know and understand the tools you can use them efficiently and effectively.

For sewing machines check out our top selling companion book "The Sewing Machine Master Guide" and for sewing machine basics "The Sewing Machine Quick Guide".

The Serger and Overlock Master Guide was written as both an eBook and print book using optimized reflowable formatting for a perfect presentation on small or large devices. Everything from a basic eBook reader or Kindle to a large screen PC or Mac is supported.

Why the low price? Electronic publishing and print-on-demand is used with distribution to more than 80 countries worldwide. The pricing reflects this new technology and distribution model.

About the Author - Cliff Blodget learned to sew as a kid repairing tents and clothing. He became interested in sewing machines and discovered that with some adjustment, lubrication and TLC almost any sewing machine could be fine-tuned to sew like a new one. He recalls "Sewing machines have always fascinated me, they have a certain elegance and nostalgia factor. My favorites are the art deco style machines from the 1930's through the 50's".

Cliff has a BS degree in computer science and worked as an R&D Engineer and Technology Officer in electronics manufacturing. He never lost his interest in sewing machines. Later he became involved with sewing machines again, modifying and designing sewing equipment and processes for the production of sewn products such as cell phone cases and sportswear. He was frequently asked to recommend a good book on sergers, but could not find one that was up to date and comprehensive so he decided to write this book.

Serger & Overlock Basics

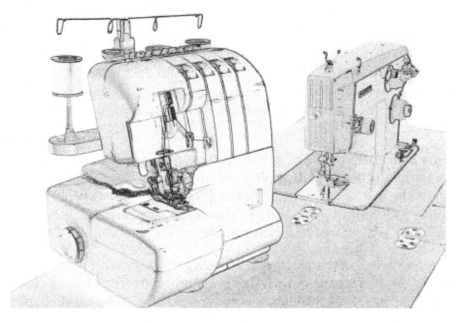

Most of the terminology used in this book is explained as it is introduced, but if you encounter unfamiliar terms there is a detailed glossary at the end of the book.

If you are looking to buy a serger there is helpful information and recommendations in the chapters "Home Sergers" and "Industrial Machines".

What is a serger?

Sergers and overlock machines are a special type of sewing machine that makes an overlock stitch. The overlock stitch is a stitch specifically designed for use in edge finishing, hemming and seaming. Edge finishing is sewing over the edge of the fabric to prevent the fabric from fraying. The overlock stitch can only be made on the edge of the fabric because the stitch actually wraps around the edge of the fabric.

A serger does not replace a sewing machine, it is best used along side a sewing machine. A serger can do a much better job of edge finishing then a sewing machine can, but you will still need a sewing machine to do straight stitches and zigzag stitches.

An example of the four thread overlock stitch made by a serger is shown in the next picture. As you can see the stitch is literally wrapped around the edge of the fabric so that it is prevented from fraying. In this example four different thread colors are used so that you can better see how the stitch is made.

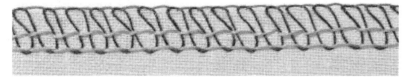

In contrast to a serger, a regular sewing machine makes a lockstitch or a zigzag stitch. The zigzag stitch is shown in the picture below.

While a regular sewing machine can be used for edge finishing with a zigzag stitch, a serger does a much better job. Sergers are also faster than sewing machines. Some sewing machines have a modified zigzag stitch that they call an overcasting stitch, but this stitch is not much better than a zigzag stitch for edge finishing and nowhere near as good as a true overlock stitch made by a serger.

The overlock stitch is made using a needle on the top side of the fabric and parts called loopers on the bottom side of the fabric. This is instead of the needle and rotating hook used in a regular sewing machine. The loopers in a serger are mounted below the needle plate in the same area you would find the hook and bobbin in a regular sewing machine.

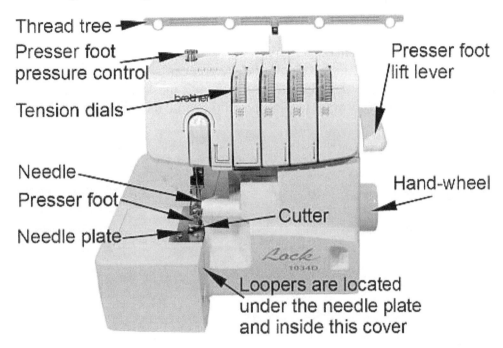

Sergers can only sew on the edge of the fabric because the upper looper travels around the edge of the fabric on every stitch. If you tried to sew in the center of the fabric with a serger the upper looper would tear through the fabric. Because sergers only sew on the edge of the fabric they don't need a big harp space (clearance from the body of the machine to the needle), that is why sergers look squat and are very compact. Even though sergers can't sew in the center of the fabric, sergers can make construction seams by joining the edges of two pieces of fabric as shown in the next picture.

When sewing garments the overlock stitch is usually positioned on the backside of the fabric where it will not be seen. If a decorative appearance is desired similar to a coverstitch, a regular sewing machine can be used to secure the edge of the overlock seam to the front side of the fabric. In the picture below a four

5

thread overlock stitch is sewn flat to the fabric with a straight stitch from a regular sewing machine. The stitch from the sewing machine is the black stitch directly below the yellow stitch that is part of the overlock stitch.

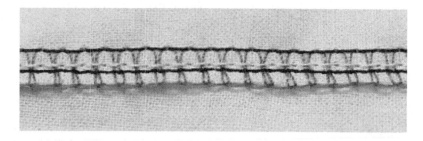

In addition to making the overlock stitch, sergers have a cutter to trim the edge of the fabric while the fabric is going through the machine. In the picture below you can see the upper cutter blade to the right side of the presser foot is trimming the edge of the fabric and the trimmed fabric is falling away. The cutter can be disengaged if you do not want to trim the fabric while the overlock stitch is being made.

Technically speaking sergers have a cutter and overlock machines do not have a cutter, but in common usage the term "serger" and "overlock machine" are interchangeable and mean the same thing. Also most sergers are able to disengage the cutter if you have precut fabric and don't want to trim the edge of the fabric as it is going through the machine.

Types of stitches and sergers

The picture below shows the three, four and five thread overlock stitches. The fabric is folded over so you can see both the front and back sides of the stitch. The front side and back sides of the stitch are similar but not exactly the same.

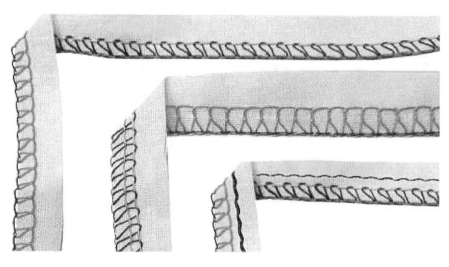

- **3 thread machines** - have one needle and two loopers and can make the three thread overlock stitch. The three thread overlock stitch is good for edge finishing, flatlock, decoration and non-structural seams but not for construction seams, because it lacks the strength needed for construction seams. A structural seam (or construction seam) is a seam that is subjected to stress, in other words any seam that holds something together. A non-structural seam is used for edge finishing or for decoration and does not get stressed, an example would be a hem of a dress or the edge of a blanket.
- **4 thread machines** - have two needles and two loopers and can make both the three thread overlock stitch and the four thread overlock stitch. One needle is removed to make the three thread stitch. The four thread overlock stitch can be used for construction seams and for decoration because the fourth thread makes the stitch much stronger than the three thread stitch. The four thread machines are the most popular type of machines.
- **5 thread machines** - have two needles and three loopers and make the five thread safety stitch that is actually a combination of the three thread overlock stitch and a two thread chain stitch. The five thread safety stitch is used for construction seams. The five thread safety stitch can be stronger than the four thread overlock stitch and is usually wider. Most five thread machines are designed to make a wider stitch than a four thread machine. Five thread machines are often used for construction seams on heavier fabric like denim.

The two thread overlock stitch is used for flatlocking, edge finishing and decoration. Some three, four and five thread machines can be set up to make the two thread overlock stitch. Although they are rare, there are also two thread machines that have one needle and two loopers and only make the two thread overlock stitch. The picture below shows a two thread decorative overlock stitch.

When describing machines, a machine that can make a four thread stitch and a three thread stitch is described and a 3/4 thread serger. A machine that can make a five thread stitch, four thread stitch, three thread stitch and a two thread stitch is described as a 2/3/4/5 machine.

For general use a 3/4 thread (2 needle) serger is the best compromise between function, complexity and cost for the following reasons:

- A four thread stitch is strong enough for most applications. A five thread machine is more expensive and complex so unless you really need five threads a four thread machine is the way to go.
- There are very few three thread (1 needle) sergers still being made because most four thread sergers will also make the three thread stitches by removing one of the needles, so it really makes more sense to buy a four thread machine.
- Do you need two thread stitches? - Probably not. For most uses a three thread stitch can be adjusted to have a similar look and function and a two thread stitch is not required.

For more information about stitches see the chapters Stitches and Decorative Stitches.

Home sergers

Home sergers are also called domestic sergers. The reason they are called "home" or "domestic" is because they are designed to be used at home and not in a factory (Industrial overlock machines are designed for use in factories). Home machines are smaller and relatively light weight when compared to industrial machines. Some home machines can weigh as little as 12 pounds. Sometimes home machines are used for small business when small size and portability are needed. They are also used in schools and for sewing classes. A typical home serger is shown in the picture below

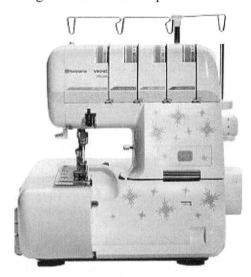

The characteristics of home sergers:

- **Flexibility** - Home sergers are flexible and can be used for many types of sewing such as making clothing, quilts, blankets, curtains, light upholstery, etc. Home sergers can sew materials from light weight to medium-heavy weight. Several types of presser feet are available for most home machines including general purpose feet, elastic feet, piping (cording) feet and shirring/gathering feet. Some home sergers have free arms for stitching around sleeves, pants cuffs and other cylindrical patterns.
- **Needles** - Most modern home sergers use 130/705H type needles, this is the same type of needle that is used by modern home sewing machines. Some older home sergers use a different needle type so always consult your owners manual for your specific machine to be sure. Most home sergers are designed for needle sizes 11 to 14
- **Portability** - Home sergers are small and portable and some come with cases or built-in carrying handles.
- **Speed** - Typical maximum speeds are from 1300 SPM (stitches per minute) to 1500 SPM depending on the model. This speed range is well suited to home sewing and allows good control of the machine. For most home sewing you would not want a faster machine because it would be hard to control. In contrast most industrial machines run at much higher speeds for repetitive factory sewing.
- **Reliability** - Home machines can be very reliable and can last for many years, but they are not designed for continuous use (like in a clothing factory). They lack a forced oil lubrication system that most industrial machines have so if you were to use a home machine in a factory it would need to be manually oiled every week.
- **Motors** - Home machines have built in motors that are controlled by a variable speed foot pedal. They can run at low speeds when needed.
- **Thread type** - Home machines can use a wide variety of threads from light weight to medium weight.
- **Cost** - Prices for new home machines start at $180 for inexpensive models and go to more than $3000 for fancy machines. Used machines start at under $100.

Industrial overlock machines

Industrial machines are designed for continuous use in factories. Sometimes they are also used in small business and by home sewers when extra durability or speed is needed. Most industrial machines do not have built-in motors like a home machine, they use large motors that mount under a specially made table. The picture below shows a typical industrial overlock machine and what it looks like when mounted in its table with the motor. The foot pedals below the table are used to control the operation of the machine leaving the hands of the operator free to guide the fabric.

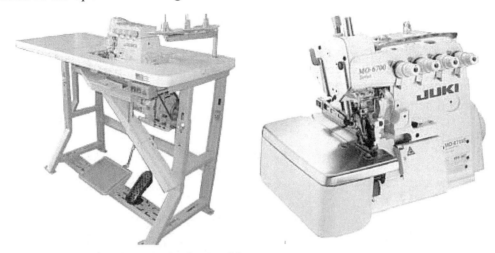

The characteristics of industrial overlock machines:

- **Flexibility** - Industrial machines are more specialized than home machines. If you are buying an industrial machine make sure that the model you choose is compatible with the type of tasks you will be doing and that any feet needed are available for the machine. Some industrial machines are set up for light weight fabrics and high speed operation, these models can not be adjusted for use with heavy fabric, so pay close attention to make sure you get a machine that meets your requirements. Industrial machines have larger beds then home machines, this allows for sewing larger items.
- **Needles** - Industrial machines use special needle systems that are not interchangeable with other machines.
- **Portability and Size** - Industrial machines are generally not portable. The combination of machine, table and motor usually weigh from 150 to 250 pounds.
- **Speed** - Most industrial machines are set up for rapid start/stop operation at high speeds of from 4000 SPM (stitches per minute) to 8000 SPM. Stronger precision balanced parts are used to withstand these speeds and run with less vibration. Heavy-duty models (for heavy weight fabrics) are generally slower.
- **Reliability** - Most industrial machines have a forced oil lubrication system with an oil pump and oil reservoir. The lubrication system allows reliable operation when the machine is used for many hours a day at high speeds.
- **Motor** - Most industrial machines have large motors that mount under a specially made table and connect to the machine with a drive belt. Some newer industrial machines have direct drive motors built in to the machine (no motor under the table, no belt to adjust). With a standard clutch motor industrial machines are not very controllable at low speeds. For for precision sewing at low speeds a special type of servo motor (computer controlled motor) is needed that has been optimized for low speed control. These motors are now available for under $200.
- **Stitch Types** - Most industrial machines are set up for one stitch type only, however there are a few models that can sew several stitch types.
- **Thread Type** - Most (but not all) industrial machines are set up for a limited range of thread sizes and types and must be readjusted to use a different thread sizes or types.

- **Cost** - Industrial machines are not prohibitively expensive. Prices for new industrial machines start at about $950 for a complete machine (with motor and table) and go to more than $10,000 for automated CNC (computer numerically controlled) machines. Used Industrial machines start at around $300

Specialized machines

Specialized machines are truly "one trick ponies" and usually do only one thing, but they do that one thing very well and very fast. Some examples of specialized machines are hemming machines (for hemming) and cover stitch machines (makes a covered seam used in certain types of clothing). Specialized machines are not adaptable or configurable. Most specialized machines are industrial although there are a few specialized home machines such as coverstitch machines and blind hem machines. In the picture below a home coverstitch machine is shown on the left and a home or commercial (used in both home and in alterations shops) blind hem machine is shown on the right.

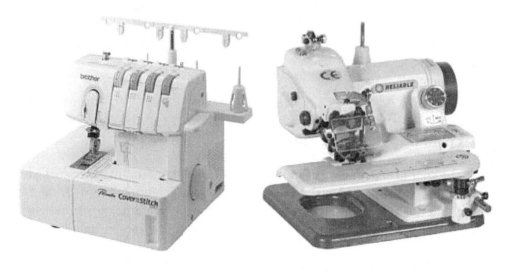

Parts & Controls

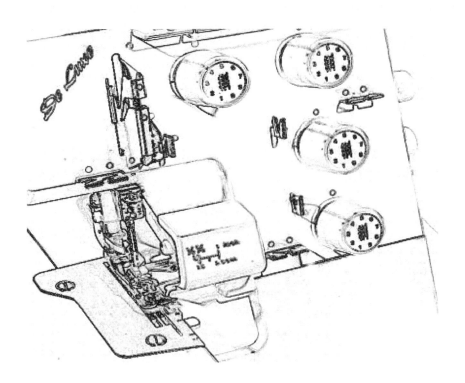

Familiarization with your serger

Familiarize yourself with your machine and its operation as follows:

- Go through the owners manual for your machine. Learn the controls for your specific model such as stitch length, thread tension, presser foot up/down lever, cutting width control, etc.
- Read the rest of this chapter.
- Learn yourself or get help? - Sergers are more complicated than sewing machines and can be daunting for some people to learn. If after you study the owners manual and this book you feel that your serger looks too complicated don't worry! Some people have a harder time than others in the beginning, perhaps you should look into a class where you can get hands-on instruction, many local sewing shops or sewing clubs have such classes. Some sewing shops offer free instruction when you buy a machine. There are also serger tutorials available on-line through YouTube and other sites. Seeing a demonstration can make the difference between a frustrating experience and learning quickly.
- Run the machine with the presser foot up and without fabric and thread to get an idea of how the machine should sound. Later if you hear anything that sounds obviously wrong then go to the chapter on troubleshooting.
- Practice and test - If this is the first time using your machine, before you do anything serious you should practice. At first it is a good idea to use two layers of light to medium weight cotton or polyester fabric and general purpose serger thread. Set up your machine according to your owners manual. Run some test seams with different stitch lengths and try the different stitches that your machine can make. Keep these test seams, you can use them later to compare with in case you think your machine has a problem.

Parts and controls

Handwheel - The handwheel looks like a large knob on the left hand side of the machine. The handwheel is used to slowly run the machine by hand instead of using the machines motor. This is done to manually position the needle to the up or down position as needed. Most sergers have counterclockwise rotation just like a sewing machine but some older sergers have clockwise rotation. Most machines have an arrow on the hand wheel indicating the direction of rotation, or look in the owners manual.

Tension dials - There is a tension control for each thread. The tension control is used to set the thread tension to achieve a balanced stitch.

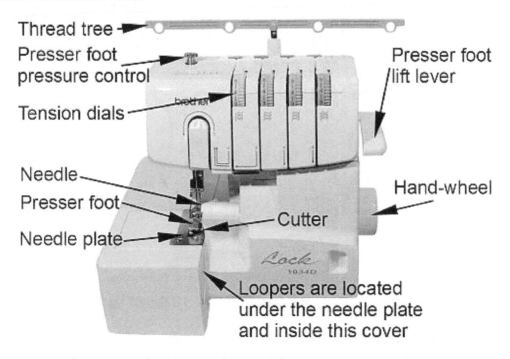

Presser foot lever - The presser foot lever raises and lowers the presser foot. Some people leave the presser foot down all of the time and feed the fabric into the machine (under the presser foot) at the start of sewing. Other people prefer to raise the presser foot and position the fabric right at the cutter and then lower the foot before sewing.

Presser foot pressure control - Controls how hard the presser foot is pressing the fabric into contact with the feed dogs. A medium setting is good for most fabric, lighter for thin fabrics and heavier for thicker fabrics or hard to feed fabrics.

Thread tree (Also called a thread stand) - The thread tree extends above the thread cones and the thread goes through the holes in the tree (thread guides) on the way to the machine. Thread cones are used with sergers instead of the small spools of thread that are used on most home sewing machines. The thread comes from the top of the cone and the cone remains stationary (it does not rotate). Some home sergers can also use spools but cones work better.

Needle - The needles are attached to a needle bar that drives them up and down through the fabric. Some home sergers use standard home sewing machine needles, but some use industrial type needles. Always check the owners manual for your model of machine to be sure you are using the correct needle. Using the wrong type of needle can damage your machine.

Needle bar - The needle bar is the part of the machine that moves up and down and holds the needles. A needle lock screw is used to hold the needle into the needle bar. On machines with more than one needle there may be a separate needle locking screw for each needle.

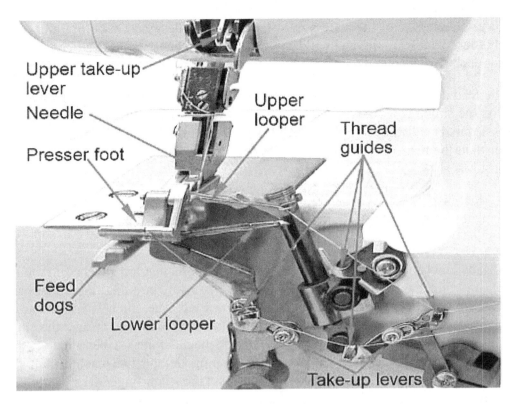

Upper take-up lever

Needle

Presser foot

Upper looper

Thread guides

Feed dogs

Lower looper

Take-up levers

Presser foot - The presser foot is the part of the machine that presses down on the fabric from above and forces the fabric into contact with the feed dogs that are mounted below the needle plate. Most sergers will accept a variety of presser feet such as cording (piping) feet and gathering feet.

Thread guides - The thread guides control the threads on the way to the needles and loopers. Pay close attention to proper threading through the thread guides. Some of the thread guides are stationary (they don't move), and some thread guides are mounted on the take up levers.

Take up levers - The take up levers pull the thread slightly to tighten each stitch as the machine runs. There are at least two take-up levers, one for the needle threads and another for the looper threads. The looper take up levers have thread guides on them.

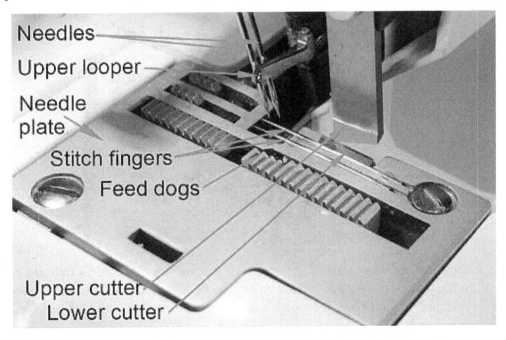

Needles

Upper looper

Needle plate

Stitch fingers

Feed dogs

Upper cutter

Lower cutter

Cutter - The cutters are a set of blades that trim the fabric (cut the edge of the fabric) as it goes through the machine. This is done at the same time as the machine is making the overlock stitch. There is an upper cutter and a lower cutter. One of the cutters is softer metal and designed to be more easily replaced, the other cutter is harder metal (carbide) and will last much longer (generally you can go through two or three softer cutters for each harder cutter.

Feed dogs - The feed dogs are moving metal parts with teeth used to pull fabric through the machine. The feed dogs can be the single type like on a sewing machine or on most newer serger models there are two sets of feed dogs, this is called differential feed. With differential feed the front set of feed dogs can run faster or slower than the rear set allowing the machine to cause the fabric to slightly stretch or bunch up for added control.

Needle plate - Most machines have a single needle plate for all stitches but some older machines need to change needle plates to control the width of the stitch and some machines come with several needle plates.

Stitch fingers - The stitch finger (or fingers) are small metal parts that are attached to the needle plate or the presser foot. It is called a stitch finger because it looks like a tiny pointing finger that has its base right beside the needle hole and it points to the back of the machine. The stitch is formed around the stitch finger. When there is fabric running through the machine the stitch is formed around the edge of the fabric and the stitch finger and when the fabric moves through the machine the stitches slide off the stitch finger and remain with the fabric. When there is no fabric running though the machine but the machine is running, the machine will produce stitches (the chain) around the stitch finger. This is quite different from a sewing machine that has no stitch finger and can not produce a stitch unless there is fabric running through the machine. Most four thread / two needle sergers have two stitch fingers, one for each needle. In the picture above a needle plate and stitch fingers are shown.

Wide stitch finger - Some machines have a wide stitch finger that can be removed from the machine for making a narrow rolled hem stitch.

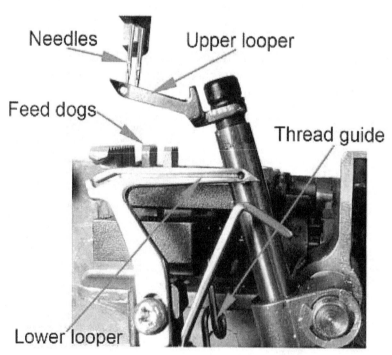

Loopers - The loopers are moving parts of the machine that mount on a shafts that are controlled by a drive mechanism in the machine, they are located below the needle plate and behind the looper cover. The loopers have a tip and an eye for thread like a needle and form the bottom part of the stitch.

Looper threaders - Some machines have a lower looper threading helper that moves into a threading position to aid in threading. Make sure that you return this part to the running position after you thread the machine.

Two thread converter or two thread switch - Some three or four thread machines have a two thread mode. These machines have a built in part that clicks into a two thread setting or an accessory part that must be added for two thread operation.

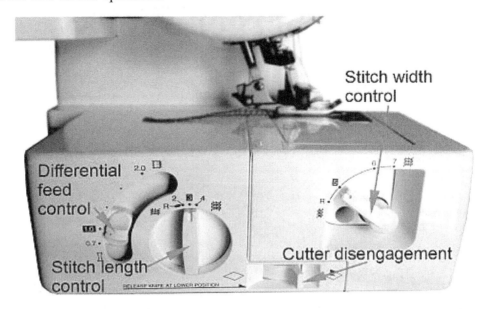

Stitch width control - This control sets the distance from the cutter to the needle.

Stitch length control - Controls the stitch length.

Differential feed control - On models with differential feed this controls if the front feed dogs are going faster or slower than the rear feed dogs.

Cutter disengagement control - Most machines have a way to disengage the upper cutter if you want to sew fabric with a precut edge. On some machines (like the Brother 1034D pictured above) the upper knife of the cutter acts as a fabric guide when the cutter is disengaged. In this case the stitch width control for the cutter also sets the stitch width when using the cutter as a guide.

Fabric guide - If you are not using the cutter then it is best to use a fabric guide or a presser foot with a built in guide. The fabric guide will help you maintain the desired stitch width. Not all machines come with a guide.

Light - Most machines have a light to illuminate the presser foot area of the machine.

Power switch - This is a simple on-off switch to turn the machine off when not in use.

Foot pedal - This is a speed control pedal that sits on the floor under the sewing table and is connected to the machine by an electric power cord. As you apply pressure on the pedal with your foot the machine will start to run and increase in speed the more pressure that is applied to the pedal.

Knee lifter - Some machines (mostly industrial type machines) have a lever that is controlled by your knee that is used to raise the presser foot. This keeps your hands free to work with the fabric.

How a Serger Works

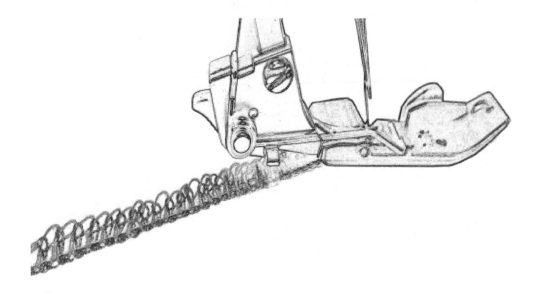

In this chapter we will learn about the loopers, stitch fingers and see how the stitch is formed step by step. In the picture above you can see the overlock stitch coming from the back of the presser foot, in this case the machine is chaining-off (making the stitch with no fabric).

Needles and Loopers

The next picture shows a close-up view of the needle, upper looper and lower looper. The loopers have an eye similar to a large needle. To visualize how a serger works think of a machine that braids or chains thread and you will have the general idea.

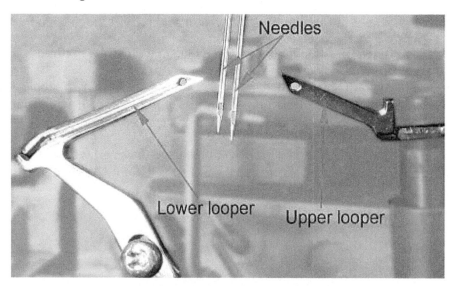

The needles and loopers are attached to levers that are driven by gears and shafts inside the machine.

The needles and loopers are driven in a repeating motion (cyclic motion). As the machine runs the needles and loopers move as follows:

1. The needles move up and down vertically and take the thread through the fabric on every stitch. When the needles are up they catch the thread from the upper looper. Then the needles go down through the fabric and pass the thread to the lower looper.
2. The lower looper moves from left to right horizontally and back again, it only moves under the fabric. The tip of the lower looper catches the needle thread when the needles are all the way down and moves to the right to pass the thread to the upper looper.
3. The upper looper moves diagonally from lower right to upper left and back again, it catches the thread from the lower looper and takes the thread around the edge of the fabric and up to the needles.

Now that we have established how the parts move we can look at the stitch formation in more detail in the next section.

Description of stitch formation

The overlock stitch is a type of chain stitch (looping stitch) made on the edge of the fabric. The stitch is formed in a cycle that repeats itself just like when you braid hair, but the way the braids are made is a little different.

The cycle starts with the needle at its highest position. The upper looper will also be at its highest position and will be positioned right below the needles. The green upper looper thread is going through the eye of the upper looper. You can also see the needle threads are yellow and black.

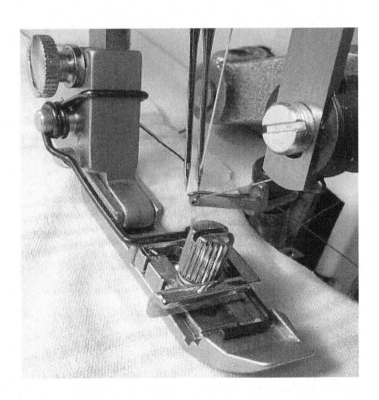

The stitch is formed in three steps.

1. As the hand wheel rotates, the needle goes downwards and catches the thread from the upper looper. Then the needle continues downward through the fabric. In the picture below you can see that the needle has already gone between the green upper looper thread and the upper looper (catching the upper looper thread) and is heading down to the fabric.

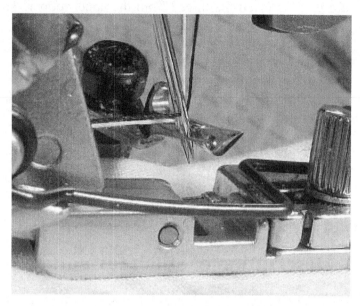

2. When the needle gets to its lowest position the tip of the lower looper moves between the needle and the needle threads, catching the needle thread. The picture below shows the lower looper moving from left to right after it has just caught the needle threads. The fabric and needle plate have been removed from the machine for this picture because otherwise you would not be able to see the lower looper area of the machine, but in normal operation the needles would be going through the fabric and the needle plate. The lower looper would be under the fabric and the needle plate.

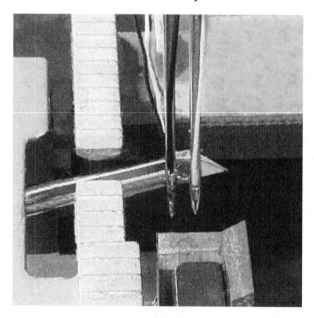

3. Next the needle moves up and withdraws from the fabric. At the same time the lower looper moves from left to right. The tip of the upper looper passes between the lower looper and the lower looper thread, catching the lower looper thread. In the picture below you can see that the tip of the upper looper has just passed by the backside of the lower looper and is catching the red thread from the lower looper. After catching the lower looper thread the upper looper continues moving upwards and to the left until it is under the needle and in position to start the next cycle.

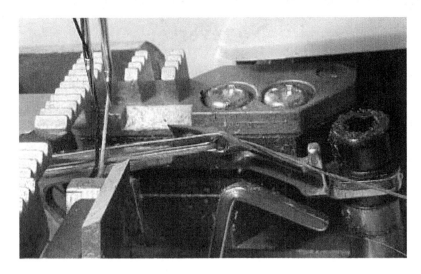

If there was fabric in the machine one stitch would have now been completed and the handwheel will have made one complete turn. These same three steps are done over and over to form additional stitches. The picture below shows what the front and back sides of the seam look like after many stitches have been made.

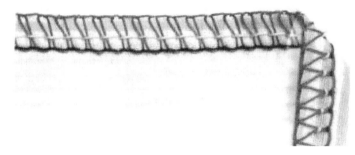

Chaining off

Due to the chaining action during stitch formation the overlock stitches can be formed with no fabric in the machine. This is different from a regular sewing machine that can't run without fabric. Forming a chain with no fabric is called "chaining off". The chain looks like braided thread. In the next picture you can see the chain being formed around the stitch fingers. The presser foot has been removed from this machine so that you can see the stitch fingers.

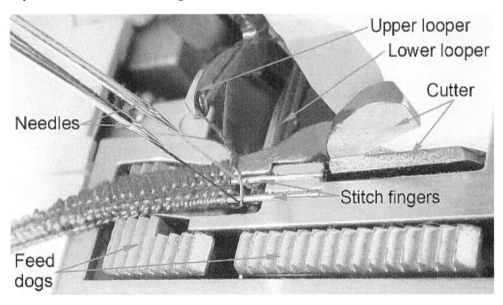

In the picture you can see that the cutter looks like a small pair of scissors or clippers. The cutter may be small but it runs very fast so it has no problem keeping up with the machine.

No reverse

Sergers cannot sew in reverse because the overlock stitch cannot be formed in reverse. When operating a serger only turn the handwheel in the forward direction. Since the ends of the seams cannot be secured by backtacking (backtacking would require reverse) other methods are used to secure the ends. See the section "Securing the ends of seams" in the chapter Ends & Corners for a detailed description of how this is done.

Threading & Basic Use

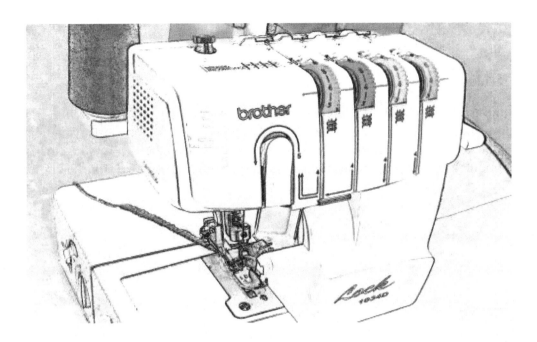

Serger owners manuals

While many people are able to use a sewing machine without reading the owners manual sergers are more complicated then sewing machines. You should read the owners manual for your machine. The information in this book (or any book) is general and not specific to a certain model of machine. The owners manual for your machine will contain a lot of information that is specific to that exact model of serger such as the proper setup and threading of the machine. If you have a new machine you should have received an owners manual with the machine. Owners manuals are also called user guides. If you do not have an owners manual for your machine you should get one. In most cases owners manuals can be downloaded at no charge over the Internet from the manufactures web site. For some machines you may have to order the owners manual from the manufacturer or from one of the many on-line suppliers that specialize in manuals.

Threading a serger

Threading a serger can be a daunting task for some new users. Follow the threading diagrams in your owners manual and read the instructions below for added insight about threading. If you run into trouble do not get upset. If the machine is not threaded correctly it will not make stitches correctly and probably will break the thread. If after you try several times, you still can't get the machine to run correctly, check to see if there is a video available that shows the threading of your exact model of machine. Instructional videos are often made available on the Internet and on YouTube. Sometimes seeing a video can make things easy to understand that otherwise seem complicated.

Know that after you successfully thread the machine a few times it will become easier, you just have to get through the initial learning curve. If you can't master it, get help from someone with experience. After you do it a few times successfully it will be no problem for you. If you are having trouble it is probably some small thing you are missing. Sergers must be threaded exactly or they wont run correctly.

Remove all thread from the serger before threading. If it is a new machine then it probably came properly threaded from the factory so you may want to study the threading before removing the existing thread.

There is no universal threading procedure for sergers, every model has a different thread path so it is important follow the threading diagram in the owners manual for your specific model. Some machines have the threading diagram printed on the machine (usually on the inside of the looper cover). Most machines have color coded marks or dots along the thread path, if you have experience with sergers you may be able to properly thread the machine using the color codes if you do not have an owners manual or threading diagram.

Chain-off after threading:

After the machine is threaded, hold the threads toward the back of the machine (pulling lightly) and turn the hand wheel in the correct direction a few times (counterclockwise for most machines) to intertwine the threads. Watch to make sure a chain is being formed correctly before running the machine under power to make about 4 inches of chain. This is known as chaining off. Once your machine is chained off like in the picture below you are ready to start serging.

Threading Tips:

- Double check your threading, many serger problems are due to improper threading.
- Use the tweezers! Most sergers come with tweezers but if yours did not come with them, get some. Tweezers allow you to thread the loopers, in most cases your fingers will not fit in the required space or will block you from seeing what you are doing.
- It helps to have a brightly lit area, use a reading lamp or other directable lamp to shine more light in the thread path area for better visibility while threading.
- Threading by "tie-on" is not recommended. Tying-on is done by tying the new thread to the old thread and then pulling the old thread through the serger until the knot is pulled through and then cutting the knot off. By the time you tie the knots for each thread this will end up taking more time than threading the machine normally. If you learn to thread the machine normally it will get faster every time you do it and you will not need to tie-on.
- Reading glasses can be used as a handy magnifier for threading the machine and inspecting stitch quality (even if you don't need them for reading). Reading glasses are much better than a magnifying glass because they allow the use of both hands and give you much better depth perception than a magnifying glass because each eye has its own lens. The best magnifications for this type of use are +1, +1.5, +1.75 or +2 depending on your eyes. Reading glasses are very inexpensive so you might try a +1.5 to start and then get a second pair that is stronger or weaker later.
- It helps to understand the function of the parts along the thread path, start at the thread cone and

follow the thread path while reading about each part that the thread goes through in the "parts & controls" chapter.

- Make sure that each thread is inserted all the way between the tension disks or into the tension slot. Pull each thread after threading the tension disks to make sure that you feel consistent thread tension. If you don't feel proper thread tension then perhaps the thread is not going through the disks properly or the disks are fouled with lint or old pieces of thread.

Setting the thread tension

- All sergers have recommended tension settings that are given in the owners manual for that specific model of machine. Some sergers have a mark or special color on the tension dials that indicate a default or starting tension. A default tension will produce a usable stitch in a medium weight fabric when using regular serger thread and a medium stitch width and medium stitch length. If your owners manual gives you specific tension recommendations for different thicknesses and types of fabrics then use the recommended tension settings for those fabrics.
- Test the machine on a scrap of the fabric. If the stitch looks good then your tension settings are adjusted properly and you are ready to sew! If the stitch does not look correct go to the chapter "Adjusting Tension". The stitches in the picture below have proper tension.
- Some owners manuals do not specify a fabric weight or type. In this case you should use the recommended (or default) tensions and first test the machine with two layers of medium weight fabric (such as cotton or polyester bed sheet or pillow case fabric). If the stitch looks OK then try the fabric you are going to be using and see how the stitch looks. If the stitch looks good then your tension settings are adjusted properly and you are ready to sew! If the stitch does not look correct go to the chapter "Adjusting Tension".

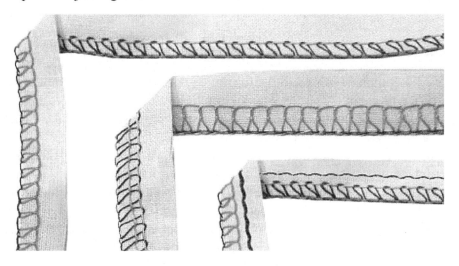

Serger operation

Before starting:

- Make sure that the machine is properly threaded and chained off and that the tension controls are properly set.
- Always keep your fingers away from the needle and looper area while the machine is running.
- Set the stitch width - Set it to a medium setting like 5mm unless you have a reason to use a different setting.
- Set the stitch length - Set it to a medium setting like 3mm unless you have a reason to use a different setting.

Starting your seam:

- Raise the presser foot and insert the fabric under the front of the presser foot so that it is just touching the blade of the cutter. Lower the presser foot.
- Start the machine slowly and make sure that the fabric is feeding correctly into the cutter. If you are sewing fleece or other thick fabric you may have to re-position it and try again to get the fabric to start feeding through the machine. Make sure that fabric is not bunched up against the cutter blades and feeds correctly through the cutter when you start the machine. Do not push the fabric, let the machine feed the fabric.
- Lightly place your fingers on the fabric to the left of the presser foot to guide the fabric through the machine.
- Once the machine is running and you see the stitch is forming correctly then increase the speed of the machine.
- For thick fabric - When sewing thick fabric and using the cutter pay special attention the entire time you are running the machine to make sure that the cutter is cutting the fabric cleanly and that the fabric is not jamming up in the cutter. Unless you have a heavy duty serger with a heavy duty cutter sometimes it is better to cut thick fabric before running it through the serger and then use an edge guide instead of using the cutter. Some machines have a cutter lock screw to better secure the cutter when cutting thick fabric. Check your owners manual to see if your machine has a locking cutter.
- Do not push or pull the fabric through the machine. Let the feed dogs of the machine move the fabric. Only use enough effort to guide the fabric in the direction you want to sew. The feed dogs are timed to only move the fabric when the needle is in the up position. If you try to push or pull the fabric through the machine you will move the fabric when the needle is down and you will bend the needle possibly causing the needle to hit the needle plate and break. This can damage the machine.

Ending your seam:

1. Let the fabric go completely through the machine and then run the machine a bit more to produce about five inches of chain. After the fabric ends lightly pull the fabric to the rear of the machine while the chain is being made. Once the machine stops you can cut the chain and remove the fabric, leave about three inches of chain on the machine.
2. If you want to end the seam before the end of the fabric you can serge off the side of the fabric and then run the machine a bit more to produce about five inches of chain. This does not look very good but if the seam will be on the inside of the item you are sewing the looks are not important.
3. Alternatively if you want to end the seam before the end of the fabric you will need to get the thread to release from the stitch finger of the machine as follows; Stop the machine in the place you want to release the fabric. Rotate the hand wheel to bring the needle to the up position. Grab the needle thread above the needle and pull about one inch of needle thread from the tension disks. Now raise the presser foot and move the fabric to the rear of the machine so that the stitches can slide off the stitch finger. Once the fabric is free from the stitch finger you can move the fabric to the left so that the fabric is not under the presser foot. Now run the machine to produce a few inches of chain and then cut the chain.

Now you have completed a seam, but the beginning and end of your seam has a few inches of chain hanging from it. If you cut the chain off, the stitch will unravel. In the next chapter we will go over securing the ends of seams and learn several ways to deal with the chain at the beginning and end of the seam.

Tips, tricks and pointers

Starting a seam - Some people prefer to start a seam with the presser foot down. This is done by lifting the front of the presser foot with your finger and placing the fabric under the front without raising the foot. Alternatively some people just start the machine with the foot down and then insert the fabric under the front of the foot until the feed dogs grab the fabric. These methods are not recommended because they cause the machine to run with the pressure foot in direct contact with the feed dogs (no fabric) and will eventually wear out the feed dogs and presser foot

Do not sew over pins - you will damage your machine. If you do pin your fabric make sure the pins are well away from the edge of the fabric or remove the pins as you sew and before they get to the cutter blades and needle area of the machine.

You can start fast! - You don't have to always start slowly, if you are sewing long seams and need to go fast then mash on it! Sergers are designed for full power start-and-stop sewing.

Thin fabric - To sew very thin fabric that does not feed well or bunches up you can add a layer of thin paper or stabilizer material under the fabric. After sewing tear off the part of the paper that is visible.

Feed dogs - Don't push or pull the fabric, let the feed dogs move the fabric through the machine. Your job is to guide the fabric so that the stitching is in the correct place.

Stretchy fabric - To sew stretchy fabric like knits or spandex set the differential feed to a stretch setting.

Chained off - At the factory when the machine is new it is said to be "chained off" when it is tested with a small piece of test fabric after being set up and adjusted. This piece of fabric is usually left in the machine under the presser foot as proof that the machine was working correctly when it left the factory or repair facility.

Test sew - Use a piece of scrap fabric to test sew and inspect the stitches before sewing something important. For test sewing it is best to use opposite colors of thread and fabric so that the stitches are clearly visible. How does the stitch look? Is the tension correct and is the stitch balanced? If the tension needs adjustment then go to the chapter "Adjusting tension".

To go slow - Most sergers don't go slowly very well. If you need to go slower than your machine likes to go under its own power then you should use manual power (rotating the hand wheel of the machine with hand power). Do this whenever you need the machine to sew very slowly with a great deal of control.

Skill - Its mostly skill that gets good results, not the machine! The machine is just a tool, you control what the machine does.

Ends & Corners

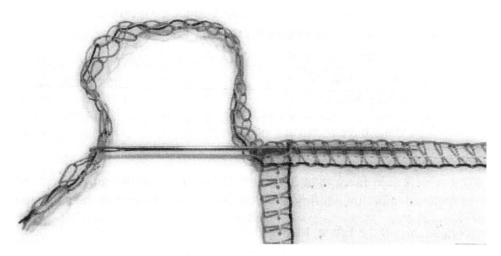

Securing the ends of seams

At the beginning and ends of seams made by a serger you will have a thread chain. If you cut off the chain the seam will unravel. Sergers do not have reverse so you can't back tack to secure the ends of the seam as you would with a sewing machine. A typical chain looks like the top example in the picture below. If you run your fingers along the chain while squeezing to pull the slack from the loops the chain it looks like it does in the bottom example. For most uses it is unacceptable to just leave the chain hanging at the end of the seam, a more visually appealing termination of the seam is desirable.

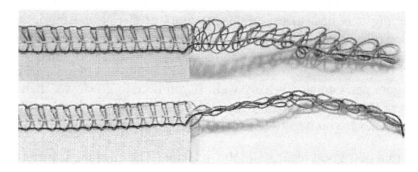

There are several ways to secure the ends of the seam as follows:

1. Serge over the chain at the beginning of seam. This may or may not be visually appealing so you will have to try it and see if you like the appearance. At the start of the seam run the serger for about four or five stitches and then stop the machine with the needles in the down position. Raise the presser foot and pull the chain to the front of the machine and under the presser foot (but on the top side of the fabric). Hold the chain along the seam line to the front of the machine so that it coming out from the front of the presser foot. Lower the presser foot on top of the chain and then start the machine and serge over the chain. As you are serging over the chain, pull the rest of the chain into the cutter (to the right side of the presser foot) to cut it off as you continue the seam. The result is as pictured below.

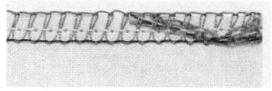

2. Thread the chain back into the end of the stitch and cut off the remaining chain. This is done with a large hand sewing needle and secures the end of the stitch in a somewhat visually appealing manner. In the picture below the top example is the finished result, which is somewhat ugly with the multicolored thread I am using for this demonstration but looks much better with a single color thread that matches the color of the fabric. The bottom example shows how the needle is used to thread the chain into the seam.

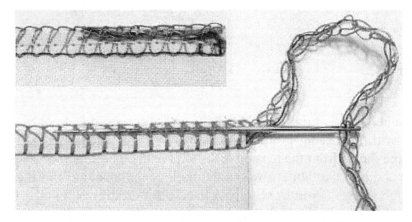

3. Sew the end or beginning of the serged seam into another seam made by a sewing machine. The chain is cut flush with the fabric before the fabric is folded under and then straight stitched with a sewing machine. The beginning of the sewing machine stitch is back tacked. In the picture below a corner and a T are shown.

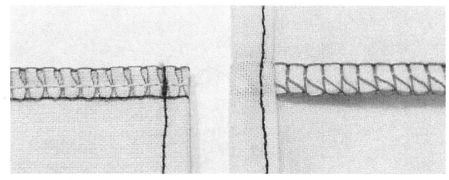

4. Sew the serged seam into another seam made by a serger. In this case the chain from the seam that is being serged over will be sewn into the new seam. An example is shown below.

5. Tack the chain with a sewing machine and cut off the remaining chain. This tacking can also be done by hand stitching. In the picture below a bar tack made by a zigzag sewing machine is used. Keep in mind that if the fabric and threads were the same color it would look better and less noticeable.

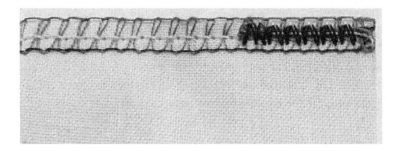

6. Leave the chain loose or tie it in a knot - If the ends of the seam are on the inside of the item you are sewing (like a pillow case) then you can leave the chain loose and not worry about it. If you don't cut the chain off, the seam will not unravel. Additionally you can tie the chain in a knot like in the picture below.

7. Serge over the chain at the end of the seam. After the end of the seam is reached continue for one stitch and stop the machine with the needle in the up position. Grab the needle thread before it goes into the needle and pull out some thread from the tension disks to give about 1/2 inch of slack in the needle thread. Raise the presser foot and pull the fabric towards the back of the machine causing it to release from the stitch finger. Flip the fabric over (from front to back) and position the seam under the presser foot and to the front so that you will be sewing over the seam you just made. Lower the presser foot. Disengage the cutter. Grab the needle thread above the tension disks and pull to remove any slack that you created earlier. Start the machine and after about 1 inch (25mm) serge off the edge of the fabric. Cut the chain flush with the edge of the fabric. This method takes some practice. In the picture below the top example shows the completed result after the chain is trimmed off.

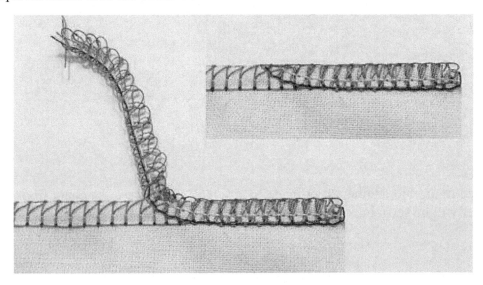

8. Secure the end of the stitch using sewing glue and then cut off the chain - This is not a preferred method because most glue is not durable of causes a noticeable stiff spot or lump in the fabric.

Serging curves and corners

Limitations on tight curves - Sergers can sew around curves as long as they are not tight curves but sergers are not able to sew around tight curves the way that a sewing machine can. With a sewing machine you can sew around a 90 degree corner by stopping the machine, lifting the presser foot with the needle in the down position and pivoting the fabric around the needle. There is nothing in a sewing machine that prevents the fabric from pivoting around the needle. A serger can't pivot around the needle to make a corner because the stitch is formed around the stitch finger and several stitches are always on the stitch finger at a time. The stitches that are on the stitch finger prevent the fabric from being able to pivot more than a slight amount. In the picture below you can see that there are about seven stitches still on the stitch finger.

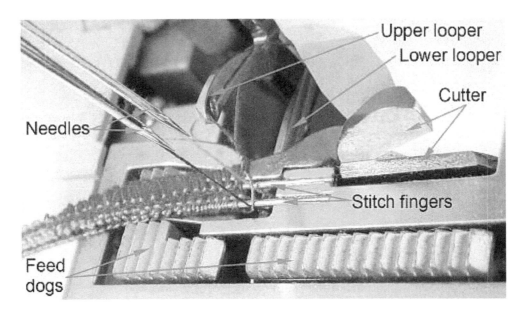

Some specialized machines (Some types of industrial Merrow Machines and some Juki overlock machines) have special short stitch fingers and other modifications that allow them to go around tighter curves, they are used to sew around the boarders of name patches and badges, but these machines still can not sew around a 90 degree corner.

Curves

- To sew around curves practice on scrap fabric until you are able to achieve satisfactory results. Try the ideas below until you get a good looking stitch.
- Go slowly.
- Use both hands to feed the fabric, one hand to the side and behind the presser foot and one hand guiding the fabric before the presser foot.
- You may need to use a shorter stitch length to maintain a good stitch appearance.
- Use the differential feed (if your machine has differential feed) if you experience bunching or stretching.
- You may need to disengage the cutter if you find that the cutter prevents you from negotiating the curve smoothly. In this case use scissors to cut the correct seam allowance before you serge.
- Learn the limitations of your machine by practicing. After you practice a while you will figure out how tight a curve you can reliably make with your machine.
- If your machine can't do certain curves then use a sewing machine.

Outside corners

Since a serger can't actually go around a corner you will be doing a two part operation with straight seams, sewing one straight seam off the corner and then sewing another straight seam on the other side of the corner.

Outside corners - Method one:

This method is reliable and works with all machines and all fabrics.

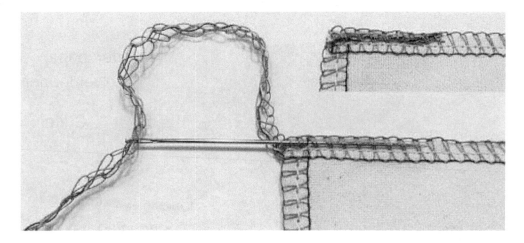

- Sew off the side of the corner on the first side.
- Cut the chain so it is about 1.5 inches long.
- Sew the second side of the corner. You will be sewing over the chain from the first side and sewing it into the beginning part of the seam on the second side.
- Thread the chain from the second side back into the end of the seam with a large hand sewing needle and cut off the remaining chain. The finished result is shown in the top example of the picture above.
- Outside corners have a tendency to become pointed. This can be avoided by undercutting the corner before making the seams.

Outside corners - Method two:

In this method the machine is stopped at the corner during the first seam and the stitches are pulled from the stitch finger before the fabric is pivoted and the second side is sewn. This method is more difficult and may not work satisfactory with some machines or with some fabrics. If you are interested in trying this method then practice it to see if you are able to get satisfactory results. A problem with this method is that one side of the corner is sewn with the fabric right side up and the other side is sewn with the fabric wrong side up. The finished result is shown in the picture below.

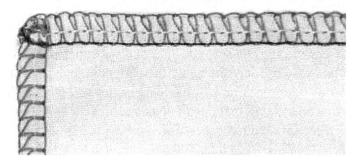

- Serge the first side but stop just before you run off the corner (about one to three stitches before the corner). When you stop, use the hand wheel to move the needle to the up position.
- Grab the needle thread above the needle and pull out about 1/2 inch (13mm) of thread. If you have two needles do this for each needle.
- Raise the presser foot and slide the fabric to the rear of the machine about 1/2 inch (13mm) or until the stitches slide off (release from) the stitch finger.
- Pivot the fabric while turning it upside down and position the fabric to the front and under the presser foot so that you can start sewing the seam on the other side of the corner.

- When the fabric is positioned properly then lower the presser foot.
- Pull the needle thread before the tension disks (after the thread tower is a good place to do this) to remove the slack you made in the needle thread.
- Proceed to sew the second side of the corner.

Inside corners

- Inside corners are made by running the fabric through the machine while pulling the inside corner into a straight line. This takes some practice. You sew right through the corner by bunching and guiding the fabric in such a way that you hold the edge in a straight line while feeding the corner through the machine. This will make more sense if you look at the picture below.

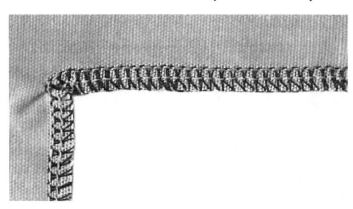

Adjusting Tension

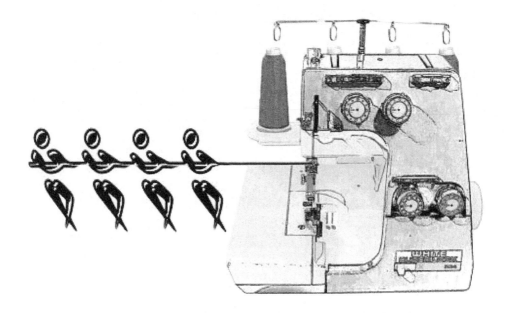

Tension disks

The term "thread path" means all of the parts of the machine that the thread passes through on the way to the fabric. For a serger to function properly the threads must be under the correct amount of tension. To provide the proper amount of tension a serger has adjustable disks in the thread path. The tension disks pinch the thread to create tension. You can demonstrate this by squeezing thread between your two fingers. As you squeeze your fingers you can control the tension depending on how hard you squeeze.

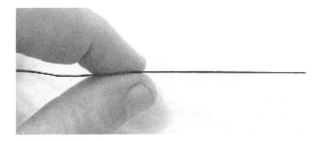

The tension disks of a serger work the same way except that the tension is controlled by a knob instead of by changing finger pressure. Below is a picture of an older style tension assembly. The knob is on top, next is the tension spring and on the bottom are the two tension disks that the thread is going though. As the knob is turned it moves down and compresses the spring which puts more pressure on the disks. Most new machines have the tension disks hidden inside a slot on the front of the machine.

There are separate tension adjustments for the needle threads and the looper threads, each thread has its own adjustment knob and disks. The knobs or dials on most machines are numbered from 0 to 9 with 0 being almost no tension and 9 being the greatest amount of tension possible. In the picture below a tension knob is shown on the left side (you can see the tension disks at the back of the assembly). A tension dial is shown on the right side (you can see one of the tension disks to the left of the dial). Some newer home machines have dials, most older home machines and all industrial machines have knobs.

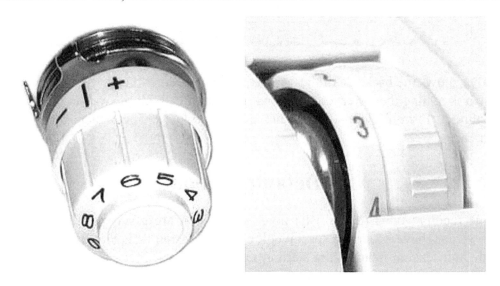

Correct tension

Correct thread tension is the **LEAST AMOUNT OF TENSION** needed to form the stitch reliably and with the desired seam strength. There are several reasons for this:

- Your machine will run better and last longer with lower tension settings.
- During adjustment It is much easier to start with the thread tension too loose and adjust it tighter than to start with the tension too tight. This is because it is easy to see loose stitches and then tighten them until they are correct, but it is much more difficult to see if the tension is too tight.
- Excessive tension can cause a variety of problems such as weakening of the thread or fabric and poor seam strength.
- Loose tension also causes poor seam strength, but it is much easier to recognize loose tension.
- As a general rule when you are adjusting tension, start with a lower setting than you think will be needed and work your way up to the correct tension.

The three thread overlock stitch in the picture above has the tension set correctly. You are looking at the front side of the stitch. Notice that the crossing point of the looper threads (blue and orange threads) is at the edge of the fabric. This indicates the looper threads have balanced tension. In a classic overlock stitch this is correct, but there are other variations of the stitch in which the crossing point may be adjusted to the front or back sides of the fabric. Notice that the needle thread (yellow thread) is tight enough to run straight along the stitch line and not be pulled away from the stitch line by the looper threads. On the other hand the needle thread is not too tight or it would flatten the looper thread and elongate the needle holes.

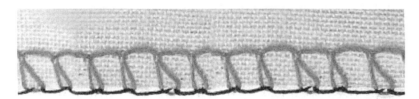

The picture above shows the backside of the same stitch. The needle thread (yellow thread) has the proper tension because it is pulling the lower looper thread (orange thread) all the way to the needle holes. Notice that the looper threads form nice curved loops but are not too loose. This indicates correct overall tension of the looper threads.

Default tension

All sergers have recommended (default) tension settings that are given in the owners manual for the machine. Some sergers have a mark or special color on the tension dials that indicate a default or middle position. The default tension is used as a starting tension and will produce a usable stitch in a medium weight fabric when using regular serger thread and a medium stitch width and medium stitch length. The owners manual will also have tension recommendations for other stitch types and stitch widths.

Most home machines have numbered tension knobs or dials that go from 0 to 9. The default tension will usually be 3 or 4 on the dial (unless your owners manual says otherwise, in that case follow your owners manual). Set the tension for all threads to the same setting unless your owners manual says otherwise. For machines that do not have numbered dials the default tension is usually about 1/4 to 1/3 of the maximum.

Setup, test, inspect

Setup - Make sure that the machine is properly threaded. Set the stitch length to a medium-long setting. Set the thread tension knobs to the default setting for your machine (see the section above).

Test sew - Sew a test seam about four inches long at a slow or medium speed and then remove the fabric from the machine and cut the chain. Mark the fabric with a pen to keep track of which side is the top side.

Inspect - Look at the stitches under a bright light. Use a magnifying glass or reading glasses if needed so that you can clearly see the individual threads. Is the stitch forming properly and with the correct tension like in the picture below? If so, your tension is properly adjusted, you are ready to sew! The picture below shows the three thread overlock on top, the four thread overlock in the center and the five thread safety stitch on the bottom.

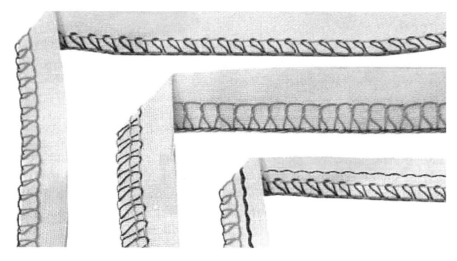

If the stitch is forming correctly but the stitch looks too loose or too tight then the tension will need to be adjusted, so proceed to the next step. If the stitch is not forming correctly check that the machine is threaded properly. Your machine should form an acceptable stitch if it is threaded properly and the tensions are set as recommended in the owners manual. If you find that you cannot get a good stitch to form then go to the chapter "Troubleshooting".

Tension adjustment procedure

First look closely at the stitch and determine what part of the stitch is too loose or too tight and then go to the appropriate section below.

Needle thread loose

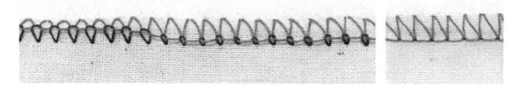

The needle thread is loose when it has loops or is pulled away from the stitch line by the looper thread as in the example on the left in the picture above. For most types of stitches the needle thread should remain in the stitch line as shown in the example on the right. If the needle thread is loose then tighten it slightly and test again. For machines with a numbered dial try increasing the tension about 1/2 number at a time. If it is still too loose tighten again and test again until it is no longer too loose.

Looper threads loose

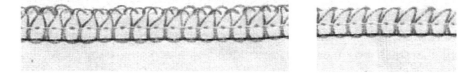

If both looper threads are too loose but the stitch is balanced then it will look like the example on the left side of the picture above. If the looper tension is correct it will look like the example on the right side. If the looper threads are loose, tighten both looper threads by an equal amount and test again. For machines with a numbered dial try increasing the looper tensions about 1/2 number at a time. If they are still too loose tighten again and test again until they are no longer too loose. After the looper threads look good recheck that the needle thread is not now too loose.

Stitch unbalanced

For most stitches the point that the two looper threads interlock or cross each other is supposed to be at the edge of the fabric. If the crossing point is not at the edge then the tensions must be adjusted to move the crossing point to the edge of the fabric. In the picture above, the example on the left side shows a stitch in which the upper looper thread is too tight and is pulling the lower looper thread around the edge of the fabric to the top side. The example on the right side has correct tension.

- If the crossing point is being pulled to the top side of the fabric the upper looper thread is too tight. In this case loosen the upper looper tension a little and re-test. Re-adjust and re-test if the crossing point is still not right. If the crossing point is now balanced (on the edge of the fabric) but the stitch is too loose then slightly tighten both the upper and lower looper threads the same amount and then re-test.
- If the crossing point is being pulled to the bottom side of the fabric then the lower looper is too tight. In this case loosen the lower looper tension a little and re-test. Re-adjust and re-test if the crossing point is still not right. If the crossing point is now balanced (on the edge of the fabric) but the stitch is too loose then slightly tighten both the upper and lower looper threads the same amount and then re-test.

Looper threads too tight

 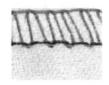

In the picture above on the left side the looper threads are too tight and causing the edge of the fabric to roll up. The example on the right side of the picture has correct tension.

- If the looper threads are too tight the fabric will roll or be deformed. If you are intending to make a rolled edge then this is good, but other wise this indicates that the looper tension is too tight.
- Even if you are intending to make a rolled edge you don't want the tension too tight because the machine will not run well and you will be more likely to have miss-stitches and thread breakage. The tension should just be tight enough to roll the edge and get the result you want but no tighter.
- If the looper threads are too tight it tends to make thread ends from the weave of the fabric stick out from the side of the seam and this is ugly and makes the seam look frayed.
- As a general rule use only enough tension to get the job done! If you are not sure then back off the tension until the stitch becomes too loose then re-tighten just enough so that the stitch forms reliably.

Needle thread too tight

It is difficult to see when the needle thread tension is too tight, but over tension is a serious issue.

- Over tension can cause the fabric to bunch up, cause the seam to weaken or could cause the needle thread to break. Over tension can also cause skipped stitches and and inconsistent seams.

- With a three or four thread overlock stitch the easiest way to be sure that the needle thread is not too tight is to loosen it a little at a time until it starts to pull away from the stitch line or form loops. Then tighten it enough to bring it back to the stitch line or eliminate the loops. The goal is for the needle thread to be tight enough to reliability make the stitch but not much tighter. It is best to use the same tension setting for both needle threads if you are using a four thread stitch, or you can have a slightly higher tension on the left hand needle.

Tension Tips

Fabric and thread for testing - To test a machine for correct thread tension and stitch formation it is best to use different colors of thread and fabric so that the stitches are clearly visible. Some people prefer to use different thread colors for the needle thread and looper threads so that it is easier to see the point where the threads cross each other. For testing, it is recommended to use two layers of a medium weight cotton or polyester material (like a scrap from a bed sheet or pillow case).

Readjustment may be needed if you change stitch length - If you make a large change in the stitch width or stitch length you may need to readjust the looper tensions. In general changing to a longer stitch length may cause your looper tensions to increase, in this case you should decrease the looper tensions slightly. If you go to a shorter stitch length the looper threads may become loose, in this case increase the looper tensions slightly.

Adjust one at a time - Change the thread tension for one thread at a time and make small adjustments, then test sew to see if the adjustment gave you the desired results. If your machine has numbered tension knobs (lets say from one to nine) then a small adjustment increment to use would be 1/4Th or 1/2. After you are close to having the perfect stitch you may want to adjust in increments of 1/4Th.

Right direction - Be sure you are turning the tension knobs or dials the right direction - It is easy to get confused and loosen a thread when you really should be tightening it! For knobs clockwise tightens and counterclockwise loosens. For vertical dials move the dial down is to tighten and up to loosen.

Seam strength - For construction seams it is a good idea to always test the seam strength. Do this by pulling apart a seam and seeing if you can cause it to fail. If you find that more tension is needed so that the stitch will not pull apart then increase the tension enough to meet the requirement, but no more than needed. To gain stitch strength you can also try to decrease the stitch length, in some cases that will work.

Stitch balance - The looper thread crossing point does not always have to be perfectly on the edge of the fabric. Don't be overly obsessive and continually check and re-adjust the thread tension for every seam. Sergers are not prefect and the crossing point will move towards the top or bottom of the fabric to some degree as you sew different thicknesses of fabric, as you adjust the stitch length or stitch width.

Tension problems - If the tension is always changing and causing stitch problems for no apparent reason then the machine will need troubleshooting and may need repair. After a while you will learn the difference between acceptable variations in the stitch and when there is a problem that requires troubleshooting and repair.

Observing tension as you sew - You should be aware of the stitches that the machine is making as you are sewing and occasionally check the tension and stitch balance (just by giving a quick look at the seam).

Problems???

If you have followed the procedures in this chapter and you are still having tension problems, perhaps your machine has a problem. Go to the chapter "Troubleshooting" and try to troubleshoot your machine or take your machine to a service shop for diagnosis and repair.

Stitches

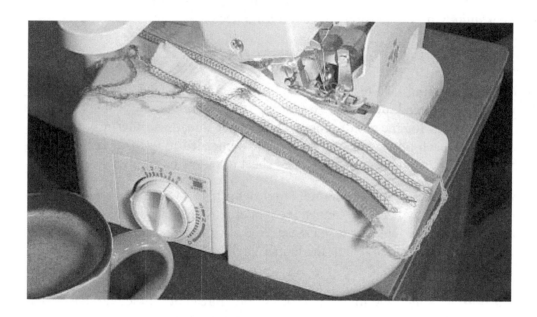

Overlock stitch basics

We are going to get technical for a minute, so stay with me. An overlock stitch is a multi-thread chain stitch in which at least one thread passes over the edge of the fabric. Who came up with this description? None other than the ISO (International Standards Organization). This is the organization that sets the standard for stitches that are used in commercial applications. The ISO also sets other standards for many industries. The ISO gives each stitch a number such as Type 504 is the three thread overlock stitch. Even if you are sewing at home you may see the ISO stitch numbers named on patterns and designs so it is a good idea to understand what they are. We will go into more detail about them at the end of this chapter if you are interested, but just remember that if you see a Stitch Type Number like 504 or 514, it means the ISO stitch number.

Understanding stitch diagrams

When you look at a seam in a piece of fabric you are looking at the top view of the stitch, you are not seeing the entire stitch. The picture below shows a top view of a typical three thread overlock stitch.

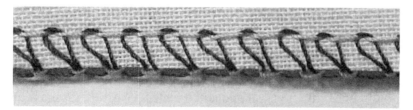

To see the entire stitch you would need to remove the fabric and then look at the stitch from the side. This is what a stitch diagram does, it is a cross sectional view (side view) of a stitch showing both the top thread and the bottom thread without the fabric. Stitch diagrams let you visualize how different stitch types are made. There is even special computer software that can create three dimensional views of stitches!

The picture below shows a cross sectional view of a three thread overlock stitch.

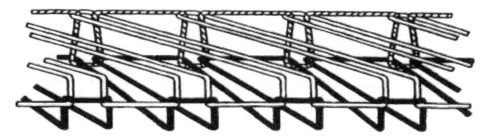

Type 504 Three Thread Overlock Stitch

The diagram looks more complicated then the picture of the stitch because it shows both the front and back side of the stitch at the same time. The needle thread is the dashed line, the upper looper thread is the white line and the lower looper thread is the black like.

The four thread overlock stitch pictured above is basically the same as the three thread overlock stitch except for the addition of the second needle thread. This adds strength for use in construction seams. The stitch diagram for the four thread overlock stitch is pictured below, you can see the added needle thread running down the center of the stitch.

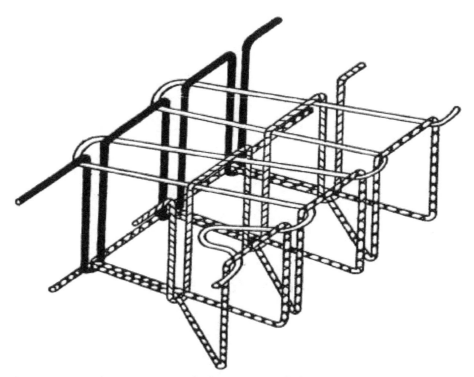

Type 514 Four Thread Overlock Stitch

Basic stitch recommendations

The stitch type you use depends on the application. The most common overlock stitch types are the three thread overlock stitch and the four thread overlock stitch. Most sergers and overlock machines are optimized for these stitch types and unless you have a reason to use a different stitch type then these are the types to use.

- Non-Structural - The three thread overlock stitch is used for non-structural over-edging. Non-structural over-edge stitch types are not capable of taking heavy seam stress and are used only to stop the edges of the fabric from fraying and to provide a visually appealing edge. In many cases a two pass approach is used, a straight stitch sewing machine is used to make a structural seam followed by a serger to trim the edges and make an overlock stitch to prevent fraying. In another application the overlock stitch is used on a hem or other non-structural area. In these applications there is little or no stress on the overlock stitch. Most sergers and overlock machines can do this stitch.
- Structural - The four thread overlock stitch is used for both structural and non-structural over-edging. This stitch is wider and tighter than the three thread stitch and uses two needles and four threads giving more seam strength. Most sergers and overlock machines can do this stitch.
- Heavy Structural - The five thread safety stitch Type 516 is used for construction seams in jeans and other heavy applications in which the maximum seam strength is required. This is actually a combination of a Type 402 double chain stitch for strength and a Type 504 three thread overlock stitch to control the edge of the fabric.
- Decorative - There are a variety of decorative stitch appearances that can be achieved by changing the thread tensions, thread types and the stitch length. For a very prominent and heavy (Merrowed type) edge use three thread overlock stitch with very heavy thread in the loopers. For a rolled hem on lighter weight fabrics use the two or three thread overlock stitch with a narrow seam width and high thread tension in the loopers causing the fabric to roll (curl) into the seam.

Below are pictured the three and four thread overlock stitch and the five thread safety stitch.

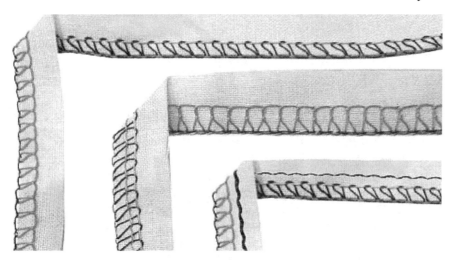

About stitch length

Stitch length is measured in Millimeters or SPI (stitches per inch):

Millimeters - This is the system used in most newer machines. If the stitch length setting on your machine is numbered from 1 to 5 then (or 1 to 6 or other low numbers) then your machine uses millimeters. In this case the stitch length in millimeters is simply measured. It is usually more accurate to measure 10 stitches and then divide that length by 10. If you need to be very accurate then measure 100 stitches and then divide the length by 100.

SPI (stitches per inch) - This is the system used in most older machines. If the stitch length setting on your machine has numbers from 6 to 30 (or something in that area) then your machine uses SPI. The SPI numbers are inverse - longer stitch lengths have smaller numbers and shorter stitch lengths have larger numbers. For most general purpose machines a long stitch length is 6 or 8 SPI, a medium stitch length is 10 to 15 SPI and a short stitch length is 18 to 25 SPI. To measure the SPI you can hold a ruler parallel to the seam and count the number of stitches in a one inch long section. There is a stitch counter that you can buy that makes it easier to count the stitches.

Conversion - Sometimes you may need to convert from SPI to millimeters or from millimeters to SPI. You can use the following equations:

- Millimeters to SPI - To convert stitch length in millimeters to SPI the equation is 25.4/mm=SPI. In this equation 25.4 is the number of millimeters in one inch. For example if you wanted to convert a 2mm stitch length to SPI then the equation would be 25.4/2=12.7 so that is 12.7 SPI.
- SPI to Millimeters - To convert stitch length in SPI to millimeters the equation is 25.4/SPI=mm. For example if you wanted to convert a 6 SPI stitch length to millimeters the equation would be 25.4/6=4.23 so that is 4.23 mm.

Selecting the right stitch length

For many types of sewing, seam strength is not an issue and stitch length can be selected on the basis of aesthetics alone. Some things to keep in mind are that really short stitch lengths will use more thread and your machine will run much slower and take longer to complete your seams. Short stitches are also harder to remove if you need to take out the stitching. Really long stitch lengths may not look good and will not be as strong.

For most over-edging a medium stitch length can be used such as 3mm.

When maximum seam strength is required you should sew several tests with different stitch lengths and then test the seam strength by pulling the seams apart. When you pull apart the seam the failure will be one of two types; thread failure or fabric failure. If you experience thread failure you can use a thicker needle thread or decrease the stitch length. If you experience fabric failure you can try to increase the seam allowance or change the seam construction to a stronger type. You may need to test different thread types and stitch types as well.

Chain stitches

Chain stitches are formed when a thread is looped with itself or another thread from the preceding stitch. This contrasts to a lockstitch in which a thread crosses or locks with another thread to form a stitch.

- There are many types of industrial chain stitch machines, some models have double or triple needles.
- Some sergers and coverstitch machines can make the chainstitch on the edge of fabric.

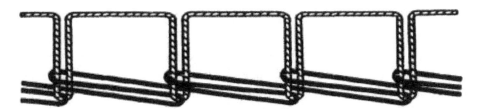

Type 401 Double Thread Chainstitch

- Single thread chain stitches are usually used when easy removal of the seam is required in applications such as basting, hemming, bag closing and tacking.

41

- Double-thread chain stitches are used for construction seams when strength and elasticity are required. Most jeans and many types of sportswear are sewn with the double thread chain stitch.

Cover stitches

Coverstitches are used primarily in garment construction for flat seaming. The coverstitch is often used for finishing (decoration) as a final operation but can also be used for seaming and finishing in one operation. In the picture below a single face three needle coverstitch is shown, as you can see one side of the fabric has the coverstitch facing but the other side looks like three straight chain stitches running in parallel. Some machines can make a double face coverstitch (with the facing on both sides of the fabric).

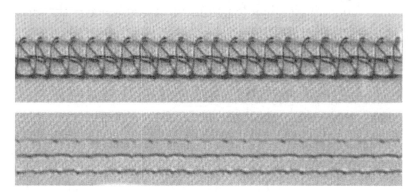

- Three thread single face cover stitches are made with two needle threads and one looper thread. They are used to cover the folded edges of fabric or folded seams.
- Four thread single face cover stitches are made with three needle threads and one looper thread. They are used in garment construction and form a decorative and functional stitch that will cover folded seams.

Standard stitch system

Many years ago the US military set up a standard specification system for seam construction and stitch types that is still widely used today in the garment and sewn products industries. The latest version of this specification is Federal Standard 751a and it can be downloaded for free from the Internet in PDF format (as of the publication date of this book). The specification has also been adopted by the International Organization for Standardization as ISO standard 4915 and this can also be downloaded, but there is a charge so most people get the free federal standard.

The standardized stitch types let you know exactly what stitch to use when you have a pattern or sewing instructions that call for a stitch number (such as a 301 lockstitch or a 504 overlock stitch). Stitch specification numbers are also used in some sewing machine specifications sheets and instruction manuals to identify the stitches that the machine can make.

If you download the federal standard or ISO standard you may be overwhelmed by the number of bizarre seam constructions and stitch types that are listed, but if you browse through the various seam construction types you can get lots of ideas that can be used for your sewing projects. Just ignore the ones that do not apply. As for the stitch types in the standard it will give you an idea of the stitches that are used for construction and manufacturing. The standards only list utility stitches for construction, decorative stitches are not covered in the standards.

The standardization system is divided into class sections by the hundreds. There are many classes and types, a few of the most common classes and stitches used in overlock machines and coverstitch machines are shown below:

Class 400 - Multi-thread chain stitches (including single face coverstitches).

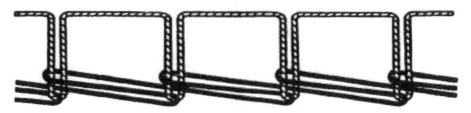

Type 401 Double Thread Chainstitch

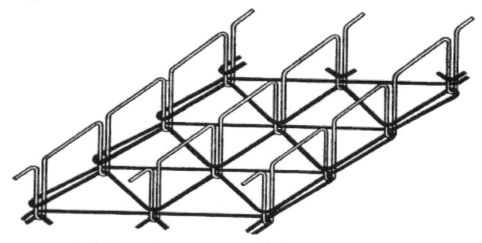

Type 407 Three Thread Coverstitch

Class 500 - Overlock stitch types (the type of stitch a serger makes).

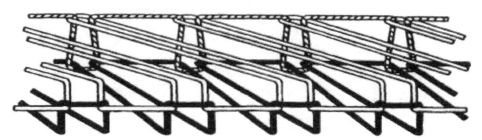

Type 504 Three Thread Overlock Stitch

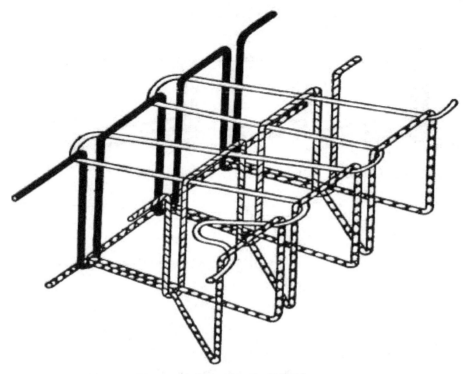

Type 514 Four Thread Overlock Stitch

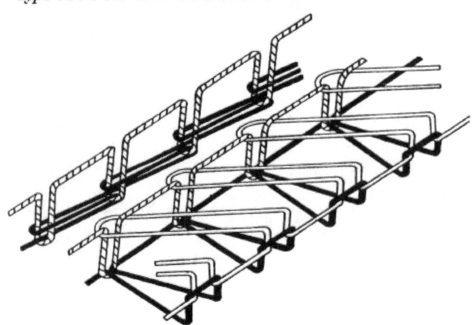

Type 516 Five Thread Safety Stitch

Class 600 - Double face cover stitches (also called top and bottom cover stitches).

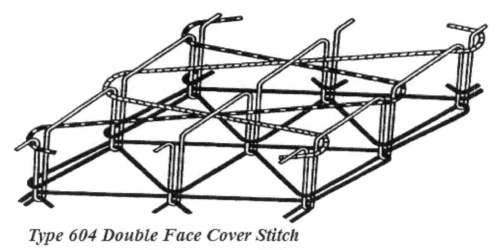

Type 604 Double Face Cover Stitch

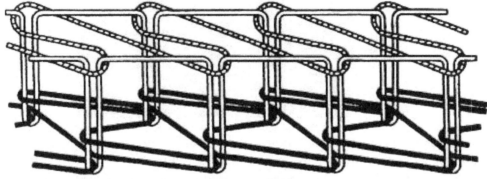

Type 602 Double Face Cover Stitch

Class 800 - Safety stitches that combine an overlock stitch and a chain stitch. The Class 800 was added in the ISO specification. These stitch types are listed in the 500 class in the Federal specification. For example a 516 safety stitch in the Federal specification becomes stitch 802 in the ISO specification.

Decorative Stitches

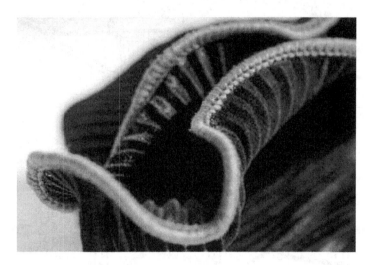

A serger or overlock machine can produce a variety of decorative stitches through the use of special types of thread and adjustment of the thread tension and other settings. In the picture above the two thread overlock stitch is made with textured nylon thread in the loopers. For the this stitch the differential feed is adjusted to cause the waiving effect and the looper tension is increased to cause the edge of the fabric to roll and compress.

Two thread decorative stitches

Two thread stitches are used mostly for rolled edges. With a two thread stitch there is no crossing point of the threads at the edge of the fabric so the edge has a rounded profile. The same thing can be achieved with a three thread overlock stitch if the the stitch is unbalanced so that the crossing point is pulled to the top or bottom of the fabric but the crossing point will still be visible so a two thread stitch is preferable if a smooth rounded profile is desired.

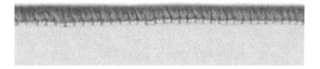

The stitch above is made with textured nylon thread in the loopers. The textured nylon spreads out to cover the edge of the fabric and has a nice look to it.

Thick polyester thread of Tex 90 is used in the loopers and Tex 70 in the needle for the stitch pictured above. Most home sergers will not take a Tex 70 or higher in the needles, but you can use a Tex 50 on some home machines.

In the example above a Tex 135 rayon thread is used in the looper and a Tex 40 thread is used in the needle. When using very thick thread in the loopers it is important not to use too short a stitch length or the stitch will be mal-formed.

Three thread decorative stitches

Three thread stitches are versatile and can be used for many types of decorative applications.

A Tex 105 rayon thread is used in this stitch and results in a vibrant color.

In this example a Tex 105 polyester thread is used in the loopers and Tex 40 polyester is used in the needle. The machine is set to a tight rolled edge. The fabric is ballistic nylon and the product is a cell phone case.

Tex 135 polyester thread is used in the loopers and Tex 40 polyester is used in the needle.

In the example above heavy textured nylon is used in the loopers and Tex 40 polyester is used in the needle. The looper tensions are set tight for a rolled edge.

In this example the same thread is used but the looper tension is not so tight so the edge is not rolling as tightly.

In the example above Tex 70 polyester is used in the loopers and Tex 50 is used in the needle.

Four thread decorative stitches

Four thread overlock stitches can be wider than three thread stitches and are used for decorative applications that require high visibility.

In the example above Tex 40 polyester thread is used in both loopers and needles.

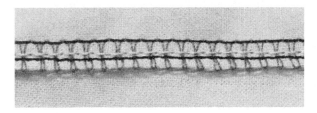

If a decorative appearance is desired similar to a coverstitch, a regular sewing machine can be used to secure the edge of the overlock seam to the front side of the fabric. In the picture below a four thread overlock stitch is sewn flat to the fabric with a straight stitch from a regular sewing machine. The stitch from the sewing machine is the black stitch directly below the yellow stitch that is part of the overlock stitch.

Coverstitches

The coverstitch is often used for decoration, but can also be used for seaming and finishing in one operation. In the picture below a single face three needle coverstitch is shown, as you can see one side of the fabric has the facing and the other side looks like three straight chain stitches running in parallel.

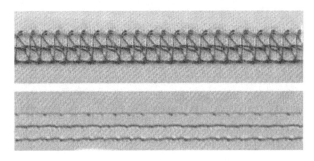

Thread

There are several different thread size measurement systems, the Tex system is the most widely used system and is used worldwide. Under the Tex system thread sizes are given in numbers like T40. More info about thread size systems will be covered later in this chapter. General purpose sewing thread used for sewing machines is about a size T34. General purpose serger thread is a little thinner and is usually a size T27. For comparison a thick heavy duty thread like a button thread is about T70. I say about because actual thread sizes vary somewhat from manufacturer to manufacturer.

Serger thread

Some thread is sold specifically as serger thread, this is usually a T27 size thread. For home machines serger thread usually comes on 3000 yard (2700 Meter) cones. Pictured below is a cone of home serger thread along side a spool of general purpose sewing thread. Home serger thread is available at most sewing stores in a variety of colors.

- General purpose serger thread is usually T27 and can be two or three ply.
- For higher strength T34 thread is recommended.
- Most home sergers will take a maximum of T40 thread in the needles.
- Many types and thicknesses of thread can be used in the loopers of sergers.
- The use of thick threads in the loopers is usually done for decorative edge finishing.
- Most sergers will take threads from T18 all the way to T135 in the loopers.
- Serger thread (T27) is available on small cones from local sewing machine and fabric stores in a wide variety of colors.
- Textured nylon thread such as Wooly Nylon®, Wildcat Plus, Best Stretch and Bulky Nylon is available on small cones from local sewing machine and fabric stores in a wide variety of colors.
- A wide variety of sizes and types of serger thread and general purpose thread that can be used in sergers and is available from most industrial sewing machine dealers or can be ordered on-line from thread suppliers. See the chapter "Links and Information Sources" for a listing of on-line thread suppliers.

Thread basics

Modern general purpose polyester threads are so good that you can use them for most of your sewing and only look for other types of thread if you are doing specialized sewing that specifically requires a different type of thread.

Spools and Cones - Spools have both a top and bottom surface (called a flange). Cones are open at the top and do not have a top flange. The thread is always pulled from the top of a cone and the cone does not move or turn as the thread comes off the cone. This provides better feeding of the thread, sergers use cone thread for this reason. Most home sergers can also use thread spools but cone thread is preferred and gives better performance and reliability.

- Home sergers use medium size cones of thread. Medium sized cones hold from 2500 meters of thread up to about 6000 meters. Home serger thread is available from most local sewing stores.
- Industrial overlock machines use large thread stands that can take most of the larger sizes of thread cones. Large size cones of thread hold anywhere from 5000 meters up to more than 30,000 meters and are available from industrial suppliers. Buying these large quantities brings down the cost of thread per meter.

About thread quality

What is the difference between a premium thread and a cheap thread? This depends on the thread, sometimes cheap threads can be OK, but there also can be a lot of problems with them. Some of the considerations are as follows:

- A premium brand thread is usually of very good quality. Premium thread manufacturers have good quality control. You do not need to test every spool of name brand thread for quality.
- Off-brand thread needs to be tested before you buy a quantity. Off-brand thread tends to be weaker then premium thread, if strength is a consideration you may have to use a heavier off-brand thread to get the same seam strength. This may negate any cost savings you get with the off-brand thread. Some off-brand thread is of good quality, just be sure to test it first before buying a lot.

Just looking at thread does not give a good indication of quality, strange things can happen when the thread runs through a serger such as shedding, stretching, knotting, untwisting or breakage. I have experienced thread that looks really good and appears to work good at first, but later started shedding lint and the entire thread path of my machine became covered with lint after a short time. Another problem I have experienced with cheap thread is splices (knots actually) in the middle of the cone. In this case the knot can't feed through the eye of the needle and can cause the needle to bend or break.

For larger projects or if cost becomes an issue, you can get cost reductions by buying larger quantities of the premium thread or you can find a less expensive thread if you really have to. When you are trying new threads, always do a comparison of any thread you are considering with a premium thread. The premium threads are very consistent (year after year and batch to batch) so you can always use them for comparison. Some of the manufacturers of commonly available premium threads are: Coats & Clark, Gutermann and American & Efird.

How thread is made

Sewing thread is made by twisting many fibers together in a process called spinning. This is done in factories by large spinning machines, but can also be done using small hand powered machines. The fibers are first twisted into yarns (also called plies). These plies can not be used as sewing thread because they will always try to untwist and form knots and are therefore unstable. To counteract this untwisting effect a second operation is done in which several plies are twisted together in the opposite direction to form a stable and balanced thread. Most general purpose threads use three plies.

Thread ply

- A number of strands are twisted together to form most thread. These strands are also known as a ply, fold or yarn.
- A Three-ply thread is made from three strands or plies that have been twisted together.
- Most general purpose sewing thread can be two-ply or three-ply. Many people think that sewing machine thread is three ply and serger thread is two ply but this is not always true, both sewing thread and serger thread can be either. Actually most general purpose sewing machine thread is T-34 and most serger thread is T27, that is the primary difference.
- Many times the ply is not stated on the label of thread. You can look at the thread under magnification to determine the number of plies.

Thread Size Systems

Threads come in a bewildering array of types and sizes. To make matters worse there are several non-compatible thread size systems and each supplier seems to use a different system.

- Before sewing machines there were only a few sizes of thread. As sewing machines and weaving machines were developed for specialized purposes, thread was developed for these machines in numerous sizes and types. This development happened separately in many countries around the world and consequently many different thread size systems were developed.
- Most threads sold for home use are not labeled with a thread size. You have to search on the suppliers web site for the thread size information and possibly download a specification sheet.
- Most thread sold for industrial use is sized using the size system preferred by the thread manufacturer and labeled accordingly.
- In most thread size systems the size of the thread is defined by a calculation that takes into account the length and weight of a specified amount of thread, not by measurement of the diameter of the thread as you might expect.
- To measure the thread size using these systems you must take a known length of thread, weigh it with a very accurate scale and then do some mathematical equations. The type of scales needed to do this are expensive.
- It would be nice if there was a simple and inexpensive thread size meter, but there is no such thing.

On a practical level however you can use a device called a micrometer to do a good approximate measurement of thread size. We will go over this in detail later in this chapter after we talk about the various thread size systems.

Standardizing and converting

With the many conflicting thread size systems in use you may want to standardize on the Tex system and convert all of your thread size information to that system.

You can use equations or conversion charts to convert the thread sizes from one system to another, but you may find that this turns into an exercise in frustration. This is because there are many different aspects of thread measurement systems that can be miss-stated or miss-understood. For example;

- Many systems only measure one strand of the twisted thread and then use a strand multiplier (such as 120/3). It is often not clear if the thread size is reflecting the overall thread size or just one strand.
- The stated thread sizes are many times different than the actual measured thread size! This is due to a variety of factors such as if the specification is for the thread before dyeing (coloring) or after.
- Another discrepancy can come from what is known as bracketing. Bracketing is the practice of rounding the actual thread size up or down to the closest standard size.

One way to compare different threads is to just put them side by side. Feel them and look at them under magnification.

The Tex system

- The Tex system is the most widely used thread size measurement system and is used worldwide. It is the ISO standard (International Organization for Standardization).
- Most thread suppliers will list the Tex sizes for their threads or have a conversion chart available so that you can convert their thread sizes to Tex.
- The Tex system is intuitive because the numbers increase as the thread sizes get larger. Some other systems have smaller numbers for larger thread sizes or the numbers are arbitrary and this is confusing.
- The Tex size is determined by the weight (in grams) for 1000 meters of thread. The Tex system is called a fixed length system because a fixed length of thread (1000 meters) is weighed to determine the thread size.
- The Tex system is bracketed, this means that the sizes are in discrete steps and the actual sizes are rounded down to the closest step size. For example if the actual thread measurement is 67 (using the equation above) the thread size would be rounded down to the closest Tex size which is T-60.
- The common Tex sizes in the bracketed series are 10, 12, 16, 18, 21, 24, 27, 34, 40, 50, 60, 70, 80, 90, 105, 120, 135, 150, 180, 210, 240, 270, 300, 350, 400, 500, 600, 700
- Not all thread manufactures bracket the thread sizes, this explains why you will sometimes see strange sizes that are not in the series.
- Tex size will appear as T-nn (such as T-40 or T-105 or whatever the size is) (nn means number).
- Most thread is composed of multiple strands. The Tex measurement is for the entire thread and not the individual strands.

TEX	10	12	16	18	21	24	27	34	40	50	60	70	80	90
Commercial			15					33	46			69		92
US Government			OO			A		AA	B			E		F

TEX	105	120	135	150	180	210	240	270	300	350	400	500	600	700
Commercial			138			207		277		346	415		554	
US Government			FF			#3	#4			#5	#6	#7	#8	#9

Other size systems

Denier (d) is another fixed length system similar to Tex except that the Denier size is the weight in grams for 9000 meters of sewing thread. The Denier size is 9 times the Tex Size. Denier sizes will appear as nnd (such as 55d or 70d or whatever the size is). To convert from Denier to Tex the equation is den/9 = Tex

Commercial Size - The Commercial Size system is for threads used in upholstery, technical sewing (camping gear, tents, backpacks), webbing and straps for trucks and boats, sails, etc. Common sizes are 15, 23, 33, 46, 69, 92, 138, 207, 277, 346, 415 and 554. The Commercial Size system is based on the Denier system divided by 10. To convert from Commercial Size to Tex the equation is (Size*10)/9 = Tex. For example Commercial Size 69 converted to Tex (69*10)/9 = 76 and in Tex we round that down to the nearest step size of T70

Metric Counting (Nm) - Nm stands for "Number Metric". Nm is the number of meters of a strand that weighs one gram followed by the number of strands that make up the thread. For example Nm 120/1 is composed of one strand of thread and one gram of that strand is 120 meters long. 50/3 is composed of three strands of thread and one gram of a single strand is 50 meters long. The Metric Counting system has mostly been replaced by Label Number (No).

Label Number (No) or (Tkt) - This system is similar to the Metric Counting (Nm) system, but it does not specify the number of strands. It is assumed to be talking about the entire thread regardless of the number of strands. The lower the number, the thicker the thread. For example No 100 would describe a thread in which one gram is 100 meters long. The Label Number system has largely replaced the Metric Counting system with most manufacturers. Gutermann uses the Label Number (No) system. To convert from Label Number to Tex the equation is 1000/No * 3 = Tex. In case you are wondering where the "* 3" came from in the equation, the Label Number (No) is based on the cross-section of a three strand thread, even when there are actually a different number of strands. You may have noticed that Tkt is also used to stand for "Ticket" as in the arbitrary Ticket (Tkt) system - yes this is confusing! That is why it is a good idea to measure the thread your self to be sure.

Weight (WT) - This system is known as "Thread Weight" and is the number of meters of a thread that weighs one gram. This system is the same as the "Label Number" system above. To convert from Weight to Tex the equation is 1000/Wt * 3 = Tex

Cotton Count (Nec), (Ne) or (cc) - Used for all types of spun threads including polyester thread. The name Cotton Count originated before polyester came into use. Cotton Count is the number of strands that are 840 yards long that it takes to equal 1 pound. A Cotton Count of 20 means that 20 strands of thread 840 yards long weigh 1 pound. To convert from Cotton Count to Tex the equation is 590.54/NeC * Strands = Tex. In this case "Strands" equals the number of strands in the thread, for example if you wanted to convert a Nec 50/3 to Tex the equation would be 590/50 * 3 = 35.4 and we just round that down and call it Tex 35

The Hong Kong Ticket system - is the same as the cotton count system, but is written without the notation and the slash. An Nec 50/3 thread would be a 503 in the Hong Kong Ticket system.

Ticket (Tkt) - There are many manufactures that still use arbitrary "Ticket" numbers. These ticket numbers are product identification numbers and may or may not have any relationship to the actual size of the thread.

Thread Size (#) - This is a semi-arbitrary system used by many manufacturers of embroidery thread and is also popular with Asian manufactures of spun polyester thread. Thread Size numbers are based on fine, medium, and heavy categories. Fine threads are about #70, Medium threads are about #50 and Heavy threads are about #20. Common sizes and the approximate Tex equivalent are; #6=T190, #10=T140, #16=T105, #20=T70, #30=T60, #40=T50, #50=T40, #70=T27, #100=T24.

US Gov. A-A-59826 Type III(VT295E) - This is one of several US government systems that are number and letter based. Another one is called US Gov. A-A-59826Type I & II. These systems are primarily used in US government contracts. You may be able to download the specifications for these systems using the Internet. They are mentioned here so that if you come across them you will know what they are. Some typical thread sizes (Multifilament Nylon Thread) in VT295E and the Tex equivalents are as follows; OO = T16, A = T24, AA = T30, B = T45, E = T70, F = T90, FF = T135, #3 = T210, #4 = T240, #5 = T350, #6 = T450, #7 = T500, #8 = T600, #9 = T700

Thread types

Polyester

- Polyester is the best all purpose sewing thread and should be your first choice unless you have a clear cut reason to use another type of thread.
- Polyester thread is the most used of all sewing threads because it has the best performance for general sewing.
- Made from synthetic fibers (thermoplastic).
- High strength. Only specialty threads like Kevlar™ that are much more expensive are stronger.
- Spun polyester has a look that is similar to cotton.
- Core-spun polyester has the same strength as nylon.
- Polyester stretches well and can stretch up to 25 percent before breaking. This is good for sewing stretch fabrics.
- Resistance to heat is OK, it gets sticky at 440°F and melts at 475°F
- Resistance to abrasion is very good, but nylon is slightly better.
- Resistance to chemicals is excellent.
- Color fastness is good.
- UV resistance is very good. Polyester is preferred over nylon for outdoor applications with long term sun exposure.
- Low lint, does not shed very much when going through sewing machines.
- Most inexpensive general purpose polyester threads are spun polyester. Most premium polyester threads are core-spun types.
- Relatively low cost.

Cotton

- Cotton is preferred for decorative stitching and quilting applications that require vibrant colors.
- Preferred for sewing cotton garments that can be ironed at high temperatures.
- Made from natural plant based fiber.

- Takes dyes well and can have vibrant colors.
- Cotton has Low strength compared to polyester or nylon.
- Does not stretch very much. Not good for sewing stretch fabrics because it can break.
- Good Heat resistance and can take higher temperatures than polyester of nylon. Does not melt when ironed at high temperatures.
- Resistance to chemicals is not as good as polyester or nylon.
- Resistance to abrasion is not as good as polyester or nylon.
- Color-fastness is not as good as polyester.
- Cotton thread can be mercerized. This is a chemical process that adds luster and strength to the thread. Mercerized cotton thread has an appearance somewhat similar to rayon. Mercerized thread tends to shed more lint.

Rayon

- Rayon is preferred for embroidery and decorative applications that require the most vibrant colors.
- Rayon is a semi-synthetic fiber that is made from highly processed natural fiber.
- Characterized by very vibrant colors, high sheen and deep luster.
- Medium to low strength. Not as strong as polyester or nylon.
- Does not stretch very much. Not good for sewing stretch fabrics because it can break.
- Resistance to chemicals is not as good as polyester or nylon.
- Resistance to abrasion is not as good as polyester or nylon.
- Color-fastness is not as good as polyester.

Nylon

- Nylon thread is good for backpacks, luggage, cases, shoes, upholstery and other applications that require high strength and abrasion resistance.
- Not good for permanent sun exposure such as car upholstery, awnings or sunbrellas, UV resistance is OK but not good. For better long term UV resistance for applications with continuous sun exposure use a polyester thread of a similar size.
- Made from synthetic fibers (thermoplastic).
- High strength. Only specialty threads like Kevlar™ that are much more expensive are stronger.
- 25% higher strength than spun polyester. Equal in strength to core spun polyester
- Nylon stretches well and can stretch up to 25 percent before breaking.
- Resistance to chemicals is good.
- Resistance to abrasion is very good.
- Resistance to heat is OK, it gets sticky at 440°F and melts at 495°F
- Color fastness is good.
- UV resistance is good but not great. Polyester is preferred over nylon for outdoor applications with long term sun exposure.
- Almost no lint, does not shed when going through sewing machines.
- Bonded nylon thread has a hard coating that increases abrasion resistance and makes the thread feed better through sewing machines.
- Relatively low cost.

Textured Nylon

- Textured nylon thread is optimized for use in the loopers of sergers and flattens out when stitched to cover the edge of the fabric. Do not try to use textured nylon in the needles, it stretches too much and will not allow the take-up levers to function.
- Sold under such names as Wooly Nylon®, Wildcat Plus, Best Stretch and Bulky Nylon.
- Made from 100% continuous parallel continuous filaments of synthetic yarns that are crinkled (not twisted like most thread).
- Very high elasticity, will stretch up to 50%. This elasticity is good for the creation of rolled edges.
- Low heat resistance, should not be ironed at high temperatures.

Mono-filament

- Semi-transparent and is almost invisible. This is good for applications where the seam should blend in and not be seen.
- Made from nylon or polyester and looks similar to fishing line, but is much softer and will feed properly through a sewing machine whereas fishing line will not feed properly.

Kevlar™

- Kevlar™ is the preferred thread for protective gear for fire, police, aerospace and military applications.
- Kevlar™ is the strongest thread and is about 2.5 times stronger than polyester or nylon.
- Kevlar™ does not stretch. This is good for sewing webbing, belts and rigging.
- Excellent heat resistance, can take much higher temperatures than polyester or nylon. Does not melt and starts to burn at 800°F.
- Very expensive.
- Can not be dyed. Available in yellow or black.
- UV resistance is OK but not good, should not have continuous sun exposure.

Nomex™

- Nomex™ is a cost effective alternative to Kevlar™ when lower strength is acceptable.
- Nomex™ is not as strong as polyester or nylon but stronger than cotton.
- Nomex™ does stretch.
- Excellent heat resistance, can take much higher temperatures than polyester or nylon. Does not melt and starts to burn at 700°F.
- Very expensive.
- Can be dyed. Available in many colors.

Nomex ® and Kevlar™ are registered Trademarks of E.I. du Pont de Nemours and Company.

Inspecting thread

Inspecting thread with a magnifier will allow you to see the construction of the thread such as the number of plies, the finish quality and consistency. This kind of detail is not visible with the naked eye. You can also get an idea of the length of the thread fibers and see the core (if the thread is a core spun thread). It can be interesting to download the specification and feature sheets from the thread manufacturer that explain the details of the thread and then inspect the thread and look at the construction details yourself.

If you are evaluating thread it is best to compare several threads from different manufacturers. This is known as comparative analysis. While only a thread expert could look at a single thread and make a good evaluation almost anyone can compare several threads and figure out which one is better and which one is substandard.

Inspecting thread that has been carefully removed from a seam (after sewing) can help you diagnose seam failure issues. You can also see if the thread is being damaged as it goes through the sewing machine.

Strength testing

Basic testing of the breaking strength for thread can be done by breaking various threads you are testing with your hands. This works well if you only want to get a general idea if one thread is stronger than another. It is best to wrap each end of the thread around a pencil or pen leaving about a foot of thread between the two pencils and then pull the pencils apart until the thread breaks. Make sure that you do it several times.

Does thread quality really matter?

Yes! In the long run substandard quality thread usually ends up causing problems to the point of offsetting any cost advantages. Some of the problems caused by substandard thread are as follows:

Shedding and lint foul up machines and necessitate increased cleaning and maintenance. Lint build up can interfere with lubrication get pulled into bearings. This shortens the life of machines. Badly shedding thread will quickly cover the mechanical parts of the machine with a layer of lint.

Poor quality thread will form knots and snarls more frequently that can jam the machine, break or bend needles and cause defective stitching.

Poor quality thread does not last as long or look as good. Long term seam strength is compromised.

Needles

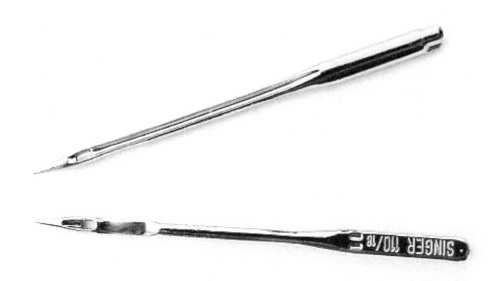

Needles for home sergers

For most general purpose use a size 14/90 needle is recommended and this is the needle size that most sergers come with from the factory. The owners manual for your machine will list the needle system and allowable sizes and have step by step instructions on how to change needles. Make sure you are using the correct needles or you could damage your machine. Use your tweezers to hold the needle when changing needles. Unlike sewing machines that have a lot of clearance in the needle area most sergers do not have enough room for your fingers around the needle area.

- Some home sergers use home sewing machine needles but some home sergers use industrial type needles. Industrial needles may not be available at a sewing store. You can buy industrial needles from on-line stores. Always check the owners manual for your particular machine to be sure you are using the correct needle. Using the wrong needle can damage your machine.
- Only use a needle smaller than 14/90 if you are sewing lightweight fabrics and you need to reduce the size of the needle holes in the fabric, otherwise stick with the 14/90. Most Home sergers are adjusted for best operation with a 14/90 needle and a 14/90 needle is stronger and will last longer. A 14/90 needle will resist bending if you are serging around curves. That said, at 12/80 needle is fine for lighter fabrics, just make sure to return to the 14/90 before sewing any heavier fabrics or thicker threads.
- Check your owners manual before using a needle that is larger than a 14/90, most home models are not adjusted to take a larger needle, although you may be able to get away with a 16/100. If you are going to try a 16/100 on a machine that does not normally take this needle then install the needle with no thread and run the machine (slowly at first) while listening to make sure that you do not hear any strange clicking or metal touching metal noises that you did not hear with a 14/90 needle. If you do hear these types of noises then you should not use the larger needle or you may damage the tips of your loopers and these are expensive to replace.
- If you have a serger that uses home type needles (130/705 H) and you want a stronger needle to

sew heavy fabric you could try a quilting needle. Some sergers already use this type of needle. A quilting needle has a reinforced blade to limit bending and is the most rugged needle available for home machines. Quilting needle types are 130/705 H-Q (Schmetz), HLX5 (Organ), Style 2019 (Singer). If you are going to try a quilting needle on a machine that does not normally take a quilting needle then install the needle with no thread and run the machine (slowly at first) while listening to make sure that you do not hear any strange clicking or metal touching metal noises that you did not hear with your regular needle. If you do hear these types of noises then you should not use a quilting needle or you may cause damage to the tips of your loopers and these are expensive to replace.

Each needle company has their own part number for home needles; the Schmetz part number is 130/705H, the Organ part number is HAx1, the Singer part number is Style 2020 and the generic part number is 15x1H. Other manufactures use these numbers as well.

Change your needles after about 8 hours of continuous sewing or when the needle becomes blunt of damaged. To learn how to check your needle see the section later in this chapter about Needle Inspection.

Buying needles

When buying needles for your machine you need to know the following:

- **The Size** - size 14 for example. See the next section for more about needle size.
- **The System** - The needle system will be a strange looking number like SA53x or 130/705H for example. You can find the needle system that is required for your machine by looking in the owners manual. Always make sure that you are getting the correct needles for your machine, needles of the wrong system may be the an incorrect length and can damage your machine. See the section "Needle Systems" later in this chapter for more about needle systems.
- **The Type** - The needle type specifies the intended use such as "Jeans/Denim", "Leather" or "General Purpose". Many times a type number will added to the system number as a suffix for example "-J" for jeans. See the section "Needle Types" later in this chapter for a list of many popular needle types. If you owners manual does not say otherwise, for home sergers you want a general purpose or universal type needle and not one of the specialty types.

When you know the Size, System and Type you have the required information to buy your needles, for example "size 14, 130/705 H

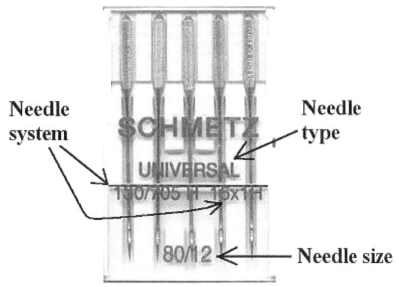

Some needle manufacturers will list more then one system number on their packages. In the picture above two needle system numbers are on the package. The first one is the companies system number and the second one is a generic system number that means the same thing.

Needle size

The size of the needle is determined by the diameter of the blade (shaft) measured just above the scarf.

There are two sizing systems, the Singer system and the metric system:

- The Singer system is also sometimes called the American system. The sizes in this system are arbitrary, but the size does get larger as the needle diameter increases.
- The Metric system (called NM or "number metric") is the actual measurement of the blade diameter in hundredths of a millimeter. For example a 100 needle has a diameter of 1 millimeter. As the needle diameter increases the size gets larger. In the NM system you can use a micrometer to directly measure the size of a needle.

In many cases both sizes are used. For example a needle that is labeled 14/90 or 14-(90). The first number 14 is the Singer size and the second number (90) is the metric size. Some manufactures list the metric size first and the Singer size second with a forward slash / between the sizes (such as 80/12). If only the Singer size is given the package will read "size 14" and if only the metric size if given the package will read "NM 90".

The most common needle sizes are: 6-(50), 7-(55), 9-(65), 10-(70), 11-(75), 12-(80), 14-(90), 16-(100), 18-(110), 20-(120), 21-(130), 22-(140), 23-(160), 24-(180).

Quick needle size test

A quick test to see if a needle size will work with a certain thread size:

1. Remove the needle from the machine (or use a spare needle of the same size and type). Cut off a few feet of the thread you want to test and thread the needle with it.

2. Hold the ends of the thread in the fingers of your opposed hands, so that the thread is parallel to the ground between your two hands. Pull the thread somewhat tightly (not enough to stretch the thread) between your hands with the needle about half way between your hands.

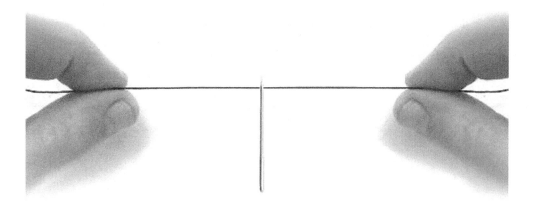

3.   Move one of your hands up and the other down, so that the thread is tilted at a 45 degree angle to the ground and let the needle slide down the thread until it runs into your fingers.

4.

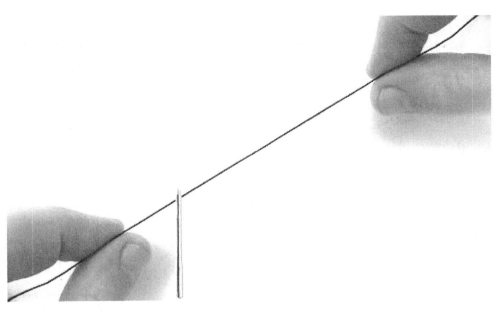

Then reverse your hands (lower the upper hand and raise the lower hand) so that the thread is tilted 45 degrees in the other direction and the needle slides down to your other hand. Do this several times, so that the needle slides back and forth on the thread.

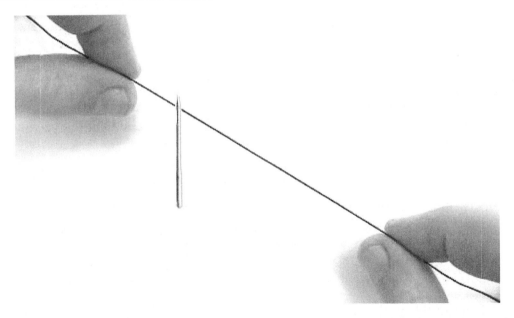

4. If the needle does not slide freely the needle is too small. The needle should slide smoothly and not catch on the thread or slide erratically.

5. Now look closely at the thread going through the eye of the needle. The thread should almost touch the sides of the eye of the needle. If the eye is oval the thread does not need to be close to the top and bottom of the eye, just the sides of the eye. If the thread is swimming in the eye (lots of extra space) then you may want to use a smaller size needle.

Parts of the modern needle

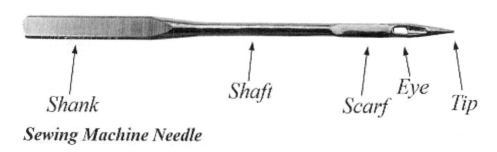

Sewing Machine Needle

Shank - The shank of the needle is the part that goes into the needle bar of the machine and is held in place by a needle clamp or set screw. Home needles have a round shank with a flat section so that they can only go into the machine properly in the correct orientation. This is known as a flat shank needle. Industrial needles have a round shank with no flat section. Industrial needles must be rotated to the correct position (the scarf must face the machines hook) when the needle is inserted into the machine and before the clamp or set screw is tightened.

Taper - The taper is the area of decreasing diameter between the shank and the blade (also called the shaft).

Blade - The blade is the shaft of the needle in between the shank and the scarf. Some needle designs have a constant blade diameter from the shank to the scarf while other designs have decreasing diameter. This is why the diagram above shows two blade diameters. When measuring the needle size the diameter closer to the scarf is used.

Long Groove - This is the groove for the thread that runs down the blade of the needle from the taper to the eye. Larger size needles have a larger long groove to accommodate larger thread.

Short Groove - This is the groove for the thread that is on the opposite side of the needle from the long groove and runs from the taper to the scarf.

Point Groove - This is the groove on the point of the needle on the same side as the scarf.

Scarf - The scarf is smooth flattened area in the shaft of the needle just above the eye of the needle. The scarf is flattened to allow the hook to pass between the shaft and the thread and make it easier for the hook to catch the thread. Most home needles more than 50 years old did not have a scarf and cannot be used in modern machines because the hook will collide with the shank of the needle and can damage the needle and the hook.

Eye - This is the part of the needle with a hole for the thread to pass through. On larger needle sizes the eye will be larger to handle larger thread sizes.

Point - This is the part of the needle starting from the eye and tapering to the tip.

Tip - This is the part of the needle that first penetrates the fabric.

Needle Systems

The term "needle system" means "needle specification". When sewing machine manufacturers design a sewing machine they work together with a needle manufacturer to write a specification that stipulates the measurements a needle must have in order to work properly in the new machine. The measurements include shank diameter, shank shape, total length, etc. This specification is called a "needle system" and given an identifying number such as HA-1x for example. The number is just an identifying number and does not include any of the measurements.

The owners manual for your machine will list the needle system that is required for your machine (such as 130/705H in the case of most home sewing machines). You should always make sure you are using needles from the correct system. Using needles from the wrong system can damage your machine because they may be too long or have the wrong shank diameter.

If you want to see the actual measurements for a needle system you can find them in the data sheets or catalog from the needle manufacture.

Different needle manufactures sometimes have their own numbers for the same needle system. This can be confusing. Some needle manufactures include a cross-reference chart in their catalogs.

Home needle systems

All modern home sewing machine needle systems are basically the same, but there are many names for the same thing. The situation is getting better than it was 50 years ago when there where over thirty systems and now there are only a few systems from major needle manufactures that have become the defacto standards. In fact the most widely used home needle systems are actually different names for the same specification and are completely interchangeable. The following systems are identical and can be used interchangeably:

- **130/705 H** - is the European system used by Schmetz and others. Sometimes you will see it separately as 130R or 705H. The "H" stands for Hohlkehle, which in the German language means that the needle has a scarf.
- **HAX1** - Is the Japanese system and is used by Organ and others. HA comes from the Japanese designation HA-1 for home sewing machine models.
- **15x1** - Is the system that was named from the Singer Class 15 home sewing machines and is widely used in Asia.
- **Style 20xx** - The Singer system. xx is 20, 32, 19, etc (2020 universal, 2032 leather, 2019 quilting).

Never try to put a strange looking needle in a home sewing machine. If you find a strange looking needle it could be from an industrial machine or a pre 1950's home machine and is not compatible with modern home machines. There are no industrial needle systems that are compatible with home machines.

Some needles from the 1950's and earlier have a straight blade with no scarf. Don't use these needles in modern machines.

Industrial needle systems

There are many incompatible industrial needle systems. Unlike home needles there is no defacto standard for industrial needles. These systems have different critical dimensions so you must use needles of the system that your machine was designed to use. A needle from the wrong system may be too long and could collide with parts of the machine causing damage.

The best source of information about industrial needles are the catalogs and down-loadable information from the major needle manufacturers such as Organ, Schmetz, Groz-Beckert and Beissel.

Caution - Some industrial needle systems have different shank sizes as the sizes get larger within the same system. Because of this some needle sizes in the correct needle system for your machine may still be incompatible with your machine! Consult the owners manual for your model of machine and make sure that you are using the correct needle system and that the size of the needle is in the range of allowable sizes for your machine.

Inspecting needles

Firstly, if you do not feel comfortable inspecting needles and you suspect that you may have a damaged needle then simply replace it with a new needle.

Visual inspection - To inspect the tip of a needle you will need a high power magnifier or loupe, a magnification of X10 or greater is best. Inspect under a bright source of light. Remove the needle from the machine and compare the tip with a new needle. If you can see any wear or damage then replace the needle. Pay close attention to the tip of the needle, the tip can become chipped or damaged easily. If you see wear around the eye of the needle your machine may be out of adjustment.

Checking the tip by feel - Some people can fairly accurately tell if the tip of needle is in good condition by feeling the point of the needle with the tips of their fingers. This is best done by comparing the needle with a new one. To find out if you are good at this try to feel the tip and then remove the needle from the machine and do a visual inspection to confirm if you are correct with your assessment. One advantage of checking the tip by feel is that you can do it with without removing the needle from the machine. As a quick check, even if you can't tell if the needle is perfect or not, you should be able to tell if the needle is really worn or damaged.

Checking needles for straightness - To check needles for straightness you will need a perfectly flat surface. A piece of glass works well for this, you can get a small square of window glass from a hardware store or a glass store. Have them sand down the edges so that you do not cut yourself. In the picture below a flat piece of stainless steel is used. Always compare the needle you are checking with a new needle. You may also want to check new needles before using them. I have come across batches of new needles that were defective (slightly bent), even from major manufacturers.

- **Home needles** - When checking home needles press the flat side of the shank against the flat surface of the glass and look at how far the tip of the needle is from the glass surface. Compare this with the new needle. If you are not sure that your new needles are perfect then compare several new needles from different manufacturers. If the distance of the tip to the flat surface is different for the needle that you are checking then it is bent or defective.
- **Industrial needles** - When checking industrial needles press the shank against the flat surface of the glass and look at how far the tip of the needle is from the glass surface. The scarf of the needle must be facing the flat surface (the flat surface of the scarf must be parallel with the flat surface of the glass). Compare this with the new needle. If you are not sure that your new needles are perfect then compare several new needles from different manufacturers. If the distance of the tip to the flat surface is different for the needle that you are checking then it is bent or defective.

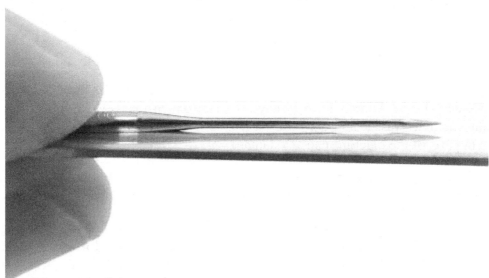

This needle is straight

The previous picture shows a perfectly straight needle, notice how the shaft of the needle is completely parallel to the surface of the metal.

The picture below shows a bent needle, in this case it is bent up and away from the metal surface. This is actually bent more than you would normally see with a bent needle, I wanted to be sure you could see it in the picture. If your needle is not completely parallel to the surface then it is bent and should not be used. If you are in doubt then compare several needles from different manufactures to get an idea of what is normal variation from needle to needle and what is clearly a bent needle.

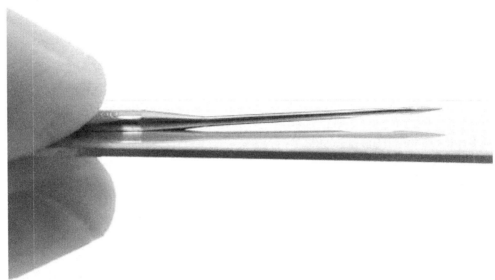

This needle is bent up

In the picture below the needle is bent down and is actually touching the metal surface.

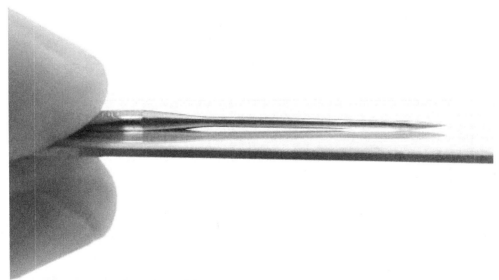

This needle is bent down

How long do needles last?

There is a large variation in how long sewing machine needles last depending on many factors:

- **Damage** - Any time a needle becomes damaged its life is over. I needle can become damaged in the first few seconds if it comes in contact with the needle plate or other metal parts of the machine. This can happen if the fabric is pulled while sewing or if the machine is running over heavy seams and the needle is deflected while going through the fabric as can sometimes happen. Also the needle can become damaged if the machine is out of adjustment causing the needle to contact metal parts of the machine. If a needle is not damaged it can last a long time.

- **Wear** - As the needle is used it will wear due to contact with the fabric and possible contact with metal parts of the machine. Each type of fabric has its own level of abrasiveness that effects how the needle wears. The adjustment of the machine effects how the needle wears.
- **Needle quality** - A high quality needle made from high grade metals with properly hardened and polished surfaces can last many times longer than a poor quality needle.

There is no set time limit for needle life. It is best to periodically inspect needles. With inspection you will get an idea of the length of time a needle normally lasts with your specific machine and type of sewing, but keep in mind that a needle can get damaged at any time.

Some sewing machine manufactures (and sewing books) recommend that you change needles after a set number of hours of use (like 8 hours of use). This recommendation is made with the assumption that you don't know how to inspect or check your needles. I make the same recommendation for home sewers at the start of this chapter to be on the safe side.

Installing needles

When changing the needle make sure that the needle is seated properly in the needle bar before tightening the needle clamp.

Most industrial machines have round shank needles so the needle can rotate and must be set to face the correct direction before the needle clamp is tightened. On machines that use a needle with a scarf the scarf must face the mating surface of the lower looper. If you are not sure of the correct direction then get a diagram or instruction book for the exact model of machine that you have.

Presser Feet

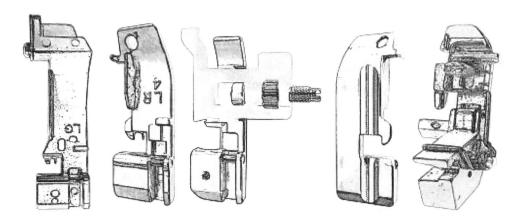

Presser foot basics

The presser foot is the part of the serger that presses down on the fabric to hold the fabric in contact with the feed dogs. The feed dogs are mounted in the bed of the machine below the presser foot. The feed dogs have claws to grab the fabric and pull the fabric through the machine.

Most sergers come from the factory with a general purpose presser foot installed. The general purpose foot will work for most sewing tasks, but occasionally you will need to do something that a general purpose foot can not do, or can not do well. In that case you will need to use a foot made specifically for the task at hand. There are many kinds of specialized feet, we will go over the more common ones in this chapter.

NOTE: Unlike general purpose sewing machines which have standardized feet and shank types that are interchangeable, sergers and overlock machines have specially designed feet that are not interchangeable from manufacturer to manufacturer or even from model to model from the same manufacturer. Always use feet that are specifically designed for the exact model of machine that you have.

The shank

The foot bone connects to the ankle bone and the ankle bone connects to the leg bone. Actually that is a fairly good analogy for the serger shank and foot. The foot attaches to the shank and the shank attaches to the presser bar at the pivot point. Some feet are permanently attached to the shank while other feet use a snap-on style shank. With a snap-on style shank different feet can be popped on and off easily without using tools. When the release lever is pushed the shank will release the foot at the pivot point.

Feet types

The following is a list of the most commonly used types of feet.

General purpose foot - Used for all basic utility sewing.

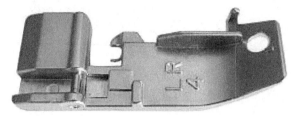

Blind hem foot - Used for hemming the edge of fabric, the adjustable hemmer can make medium to wide hems. The blind hem foot can also be used for flatlocking and pin tucking.

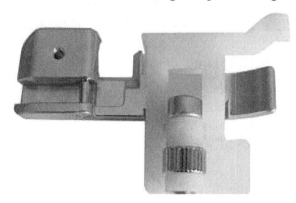

Cording and piping foot - Used for attaching cording and piping. In the picture below the bottom side of the foot is shown so that you can see the channel.

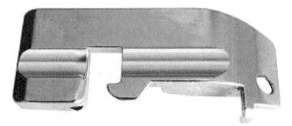

This channel runs from front to the back for the the cording or piping to go through. The channel helps center the needle perfectly on the edge of the piping as the piping goes through the foot.

Gathering foot - Used for gathering.

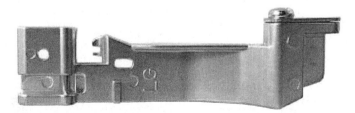

The amount of gathering is controlled by the differential feed control and the stitch length of the machine, a longer stitch length results in more gathering.

Home Sergers

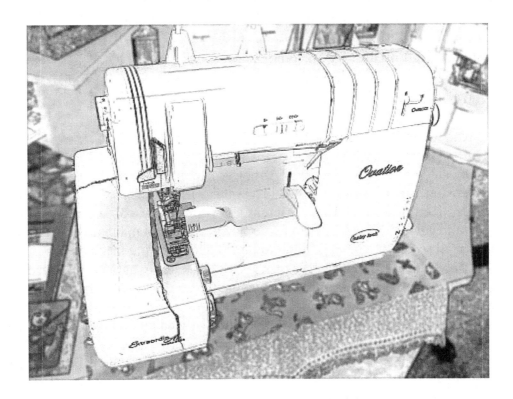

This chapter has general information about home sergers and gives an overview of some home serger models that are now in production. The recommendations given in this chapter are my recommendations and opinions. Compare them with your requirements and decide what will work for you. I have no connection of any kind with the companies that make these machines. My criteria for recommending machines is value, reliability, ease of use and flexibility. New models are being introduced all the time so check those out as well. The model numbers for these machines are the ones sold in the USA and are 120 volt machines, in your country similar machines may be sold with different model numbers and use a different voltage. The prices that are listed were at the time of writing of the book and may change.

First, a word about inexpensive sergers - Online sellers like Amazon and large discount stores like Walmart can sell inexpensive machines and make a profit. Most local sewing stores do not like inexpensive machines because they can't make a profit from the sale or service of these machines. Some local stores and smaller chain stores spread misinformation about inexpensive machines in an attempt to cause customers to buy a more expensive machine. These stores tell customers that inexpensive machines are of bad quality and will break or will give inferior stitch quality. Unfortunately this is so widespread that some of the people who work for these stores honestly believe this misinformation. The blanket statement that all inexpensive machines are bad is false. Inexpensive machines from major brands like Brother and Singer are usually very good machines.

Features & Capabilities

This is a general checklist of features and items that you may find are important for your type of sewing. See the glossary at the end of the book for a definition of any of these terms.

- **Top Speed** - Home sergers run at 1300 to 1500 SPM (stitches per minute). This is much faster than you would think because a serger makes a complete stitch every cycle. In contrast a sewing machine takes two cycles to make an overedge stitch. If a fast home sewing machine can sew normal stitching at 1000 SPM the same machine could only sew an overedge stitch at 500 SPM. This means that the serger would be about three times faster than the domestic sewing machine. This is because the serger has one needle and two loopers that are all forming the stitch at the same time whereas the sewing machine needle has to do all the work when a sewing machine makes the overedge stitch.
- **Stitches, threads and needles** - Most common are:
    - 2 thread (1 needle) Overlock stitch.
    - 3 thread (1 needle) Overlock stitch.
    - 4 thread (2 needle) Overlock stitch.
    - 5 thread (2 needle) Safety stitch.
- **Easy threading** - Most newer models are not too difficult to thread and some have various features to make threading easier like gizmos to help thread the lower looper. Some older machines were much more difficult to thread and this was a problem when the thread needed to be changed often like for projects using different color threads. If you are worried about threading difficulty try threading the machine before you buy it. Keep in mind that with practice it gets much easier but that all sergers are more difficult to thread than a sewing machine.
- **Automatic threading** - Some very expensive models have automatic threading. Most auto threading machines use compressed air to move the thread through the machine to achieve this. In my opinion the added cost and complexity is not worth the convenience, but you should make your own decision about this. If you are frequently changing thread colors this can be an advantage.
- **Numbered tension dials** - All new machines now have numbered tension dials so that you can make notes about what tension settings worked well for different combinations of thread and fabric and then reset those tensions at a later time.
- **Easy to operate controls** - Some models are laid out with the controls in locations that make them easier to operate. For instance some models have the presser foot lifter on the right hand side of the machine, this leaves the left hand free to guide the fabric through the machine.
- **Differential feed** - Most newer machines have differential feed. Differential feed uses two separate feed dogs, one in front of the needle and one behind the needle. These feed dogs can be set to run at different speeds. If the front dogs are running faster than the rear dogs the fabric will bunch. If the front dogs are running slower than the rear dogs the fabric will stretch. In this way the feed can be adjusted for any type of fabric including difficult stretch fabrics that would be very hard to sew normally. This is a big advantage when sewing hard to handle fabrics such as knits or fabrics with slippery surfaces.
- **Stitch width and stitch length** - All new machines that I have seen recently have an acceptable range of stitch widths and stitch lengths but some older machines were limited. Most newer machines can vary the stitch width from 3mm to 7mm and the stitch length from .8mm to 4mm.
- **Free arm** - Good to have if you are sewing sleeves and cuffs. Most newer home sergers have a free arm.
- **Robustness** - Some machines are quite heavy-duty and can handle many layers of thick fabric and very thick threads in the loopers, other machines do not do so well with thick fabrics or threads. Unlike home sewing machines where there are specific heavy-duty models there are no home sergers that are specifically marketed as heavy-duty. This means that if you are going to sew thick fabrics or use thick threads you should test the machine before buying it to make sure that it can live up to your expectations. I have noted my experiences with a few machines in the following list of machines that are quite heavy-duty, the other machines I did not test with thick fabrics or thread so you should test them your self if you are interested in those machines.
- **Feet and accessories** - Some machines are sold with several feet and accessories, this can save

time and money later if you need these feet and accessories.

- **Computer and LCD** - Some high end models are electronic machines and have built in computers with an LCD display. In my opinion the added cost and complexity is not worth any features or convenience that a computer could add to a serger, but you should make your own decision about this.
- **Adjustable presser foot pressure** - This helps to adjust the feed to the type of fabric you are using.
- **Knee lifter** - Allows the presser foot to be lifted by a lever with your knee so that both hands can be used to guide the fabric. Most industrial overlock machines have a knee lifter, most home machines do not.

New Machines

These new machines are the best value in their price range and are all good machines. If you are new to serging and are not technically proficient, you may find threading a serger difficult. If this is the case consider the Brother 1034D, Brother DZ1234, Singer 14J250 or Viking 200S models. These models may be easier to thread for new users. If you are not sure, take some time and go to a store and try out the machines you are interested in to make sure.

Brother 1034D ($191 on Amazon) - This is a very good 3/4 thread serger at a low price, very reliable and easy to thread. Handles all types of fabrics including heavy fabrics and multiple layers. In my experience this is the best machine available the low price range. Handles large size looper threads for decorative stitches. Has both cutters mounted in the machine bed for improved visibility in the needle area. The upper cutter can lock into the low position when not being used and becomes a fabric guide. The pressure foot lift handle is of the right side of machine so your left hand can be used to position the fabric. Max speed is 1300 SPM. Color coded threading, adjustable presser foot pressure. Uses regular home type needles (130/705 H).

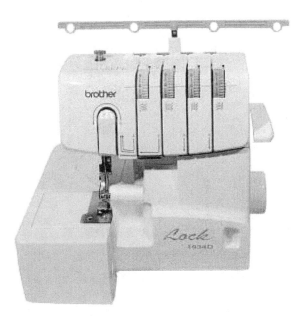

Brother DZ1234 ($229 on Amazon) - Same as the Brother 1034D but comes with extra feet.

Singer 14CG754 ($189 on Amazon) - This is a 2/3/4 thread serger at a low price. Good for light to medium weight work, not as strong or as easy to thread as the Brother 1034D. The Singer 14SH654 is similar but is a 3/4 thread machine. I have included the 14CG754 in this book because it is low cost, widely available, and will make the two thread stitches (if you need them). Some first time users that find this machine hard to thread, experienced users do not have this problem. Max speed is 1300 SPM.

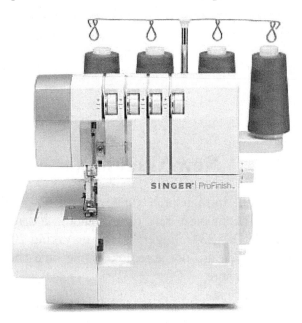

Singer 14J250 ($279 on Amazon) - 2/3/4 thread serger with easy access to loopers. This machine has an opening front assembly that gives full access to the lower looper for easy threading, so it is easy to thread and easy to clean. Well built machine good for light to heavy fabrics.

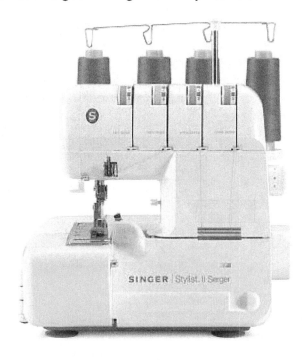

Janome 8002D ($299 on Amazon) - 3/4 thread serger. Great work horse machine for any fabric weight.

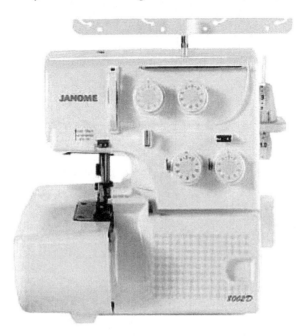

Juki MO-644D ($299 on-line dealers) - This is a 2/3/4 thread model. Great work horse machine for any fabric weight. The two thread converter that is needed to make the two thread stitches is an optional part on this machine and must be ordered separately. Max speed is 1500 SPM, Differential feed, stitch length 1mm to 4mm, stitch width 2mm for rolled hem and 4mm to 6mm overlock stitches, color coded threading, adjustable presser foot pressure. Juki makes high quality machines, all of their models are very good. Uses regular home type needles (130/705 H).

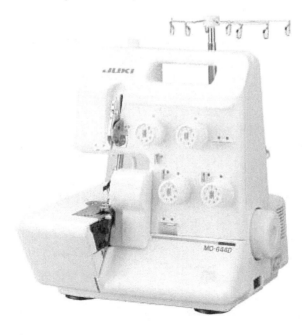

Janome Magnolia 7034D ($399 on Amazon) 3/4 thread serger. Great work horse machine for any fabric weight.

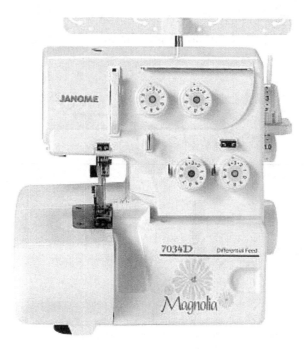

Juki MO-654DE ($397 on Amazon) - This is a 2/3/4 thread model that comes with many feet and accessories. Great work horse machine for any fabric weight. Max speed is 1500 SPM, Differential feed, stitch length 1mm to 4mm, stitch width 2mm for rolled hem and 4mm to 6mm overlock stitches, color coded threading, adjustable presser foot pressure. Juki makes high quality machines, all of their models are very good. Uses regular home type needles (130/705 H).

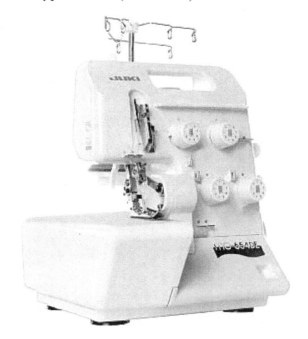

Baby Lock Lauren (about $429 in sewing stores) - Great basic2/3/4 thread work horse machine. Many of the stores that sell this machine will include instruction on how to use the machine. This can be good for anyone who is worried about getting started with a serger.

Singer 14T968DC ($419 on Amazon) - 2/3/4/5 thread serger, that can also make a coverstitch. This machine has a lot of capabilities for the price! If you are technically proficient you will have no problem, but if your not the learning curve for this machine may be a problem for you. Has good documentation and workbooks available on the Singer web site.

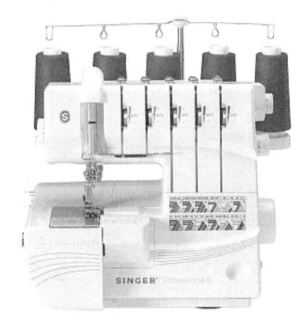

Viking 200S ($499 in stores) - Same as Singer 14J250 but sold through Viking dealers. Most Viking dealers offer instruction.

Juki MO-655 ($599 on line dealers) - This is a 2/3/4/5 thread machine that will also make a two thread chain stitch. Max speed is 1500 SPM, Differential feed, stitch length 1mm to 4mm, stitch width 2mm for rolled hem, 4mm to 6mm overlock stitches and 10mm for the chain and safety stitches, color coded threading, adjustable presser foot pressure. Juki makes high quality machines, all of their models are very good. Uses regular home type needles (130/705 H).

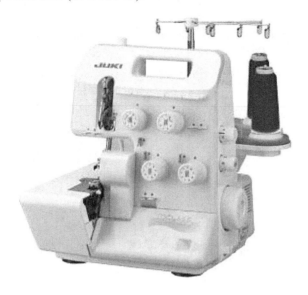

Juki MO-735 ($899 on-line dealers) - This is a 2/3/4/5 thread serger that will also make a two or three needle cover stitch and a two thread chain stitch. Max speed is 1500 SPM, Differential feed, stitch length 1mm to 4mm, stitch width 2mm for rolled hem, 5mm to 7mm overlock stitches and 10mm for the chain and safety stitches, color coded threading, adjustable presser foot pressure. Juki makes high quality machines, all of their models are very good. Uses regular home type needles (130/705 H).

Expensive Machines ($1000 to $5000) - Baby Lock, Juki, Brother, Janome, Pfaff, Viking and other companies all make expensive machines. Most of these machines work great if you can afford them. Just make sure that you really need the bells and whistles (extra features) and that the cost makes sense to you. Remember all machines can make a good looking stitch!

Used machines

Unless you can get a used serger in very good condition at a very good price then get a new serger. Used sergers get expensive quickly if you have to take them to the repair shop. You can spend more on a used serger and a single visit to the repair shop then a new serger will cost. On the other hand if you are getting a great deal and you are sure that the used machine is in good condition then a used machine may be worth considering.

Some ideas

Simple is good! - If you are not sure what type of machine is best for you, get a basic inexpensive machine and save yourself some money. The stitch quality of all machines is about the same if they are adjusted properly and are in good condition. Most industrial machines used by seamstresses, tailors and in factories are basic machines. Proficient sewing is achieved through skill. An expensive machine with automatic features wont make up for a lack of knowledge and skill.

Stitch selection - A large selection of stitches is not important! Ninety five percent of all sewing is done with a few basic stitch types, but because this is not well understood, many people buy machines with as many stitches as possible.

For general use get a 4 thread (2 needle) serger. You will need a 4 thread (2 needle) serger for construction seams (structural seams) because the fourth thread forms a second stitch line that makes the stitch much stronger. Three threads are good for edge finishing and non-structural seams but not for construction seams. There are very few 3 thread (1 needle) home sergers still being made because a 4 thread serger will also make a 3 thread stitch by removing one of the needles, so it makes sense to buy a 4 thread machine.

Five thread stitches are slightly stronger than a 4 thread stitch but for most sewing a 4 thread stitch works fine and the added expense and complexity of a 5 thread machine is not normally needed. You can also add another stitch line to a 3 thread overlock stitch using a straight stitch sewing machine if you need a 5 thread safety stitch occasionally.

Coverstitch - Some models of sergers will also make the coverstitch. If you need to sew with a coverstitch one of these machines may be a good idea or alternatively you can get an inexpensive serger and an inexpensive coverstitch machine for about the same cost. For more information about coverstitch machines see the chapter "Coverstitch Machines" later in the book.

Machine adjustment - The correct needle, thread and adjustment of a machine makes a huge difference, more difference then the brand and model of machine. An improperly adjusted $2000 machine will sew considerably worse than a properly adjusted $190 machine. Learning how to troubleshoot a serger is not difficult and will add tremendously to a positive sewing experience.

Do you really need a serger? You can use a zigzag sewing machine for edge finishing (using a zigzag stitch or an overedge stitch). If you need to stitch and cut the edge of the fabric at the same time (like a serger does), you can buy an edge cutting foot for your zigzag sewing machine. The down side to using a zigzag machine for edge finishing is slow speed and poorer stitch quality. The overedge stitch does not look as good as a real overlock stitch. If you need to do edge finishing only occasionally then try using your sewing machine before buying a serger, it may work for you. If you don't like the results then get a serger.

If you already have a sewing machine and want to expand your capabilities, a serger may be a good addition to your sewing setup. Generally a serger does not replace a sewing machine, you will still need a sewing machine for straight stitching and zigzag stitching.

How to test machines and do research

First do your research on the Internet. Before you go to a sewing machine dealer and try out machines you should research the machines you are interested in and read user feedback and comments. This is very important because it takes a while to really know a serger. During a quick test you may think that you really like a machine only to find that after a few months you don't like it. This can be avoided by reading as much as you can about the machines you are interested in. If you find that a certain machine is overwhelmingly liked by users then it is a good bet that you will like it. Or you may read about certain issues with a machine that need further consideration.

Go on-line and download the user manuals for the machines you are interested in. If the manuals are not available on-line then the manufacturer may be hiding something or does not want you to do a direct comparison of their products. Reading the user manual can give you a good amount of information about the machine that you will not find elsewhere.

Be careful about getting opinions from users that have just bought a new machine and are trying to convince themselves that they made a good purchase but have not extensively used the machine yet. Ask them how long they have had the machine and what they have actually done with it. This includes on-line opinions.

Test sew the machines if you can. Also go through threading the machine, some machines are overly difficult to thread. Bring the type of fabric and thread that you use for your projects. Do as much sewing on the machines as possible. Try out all of the features that you are most concerned with. Take notes if you are testing several machines. If you know what the most troublesome operations are for you, then try those operations with the machines you are testing.

Vintage & Classic Sergers

The first home sergers started to appear in the late 1960's and were made by Juki, the famous manufacturer of industrial machines. These machines were sold under many names such as the "SO-FRO" in the picture above. These were solid reliable machines, many of them are still running today after many years of use.

Besides adding some features there has been little functional change in home sergers in the last 40 years. Most domestic sergers are still made by a few manufactures and then sold under many brands. Some of the manufacturers that make domestic sergers are Juki, Jaguar, Brother and Janome. If you don't recognize Jaguar, this is the manufacturer that made the Kenmore sewing machines with the solid aluminum body parts up until the 1980's. Most brand name companies that sell sewing machines also sell sergers including Singer, Brother, Janome, Bernina, Elna, Pfaff, Viking and Baby Lock.

Classic Machines

Juki made several early models and also manufactured similar models for Baby Lock. I am including them in the book because they made a lot of these and if you do find one in good condition at a low price they can be a good workhorse machine. Don't forget that a new Brother 1034D (see the chapter Home Sergers) costs $191 on Amazon so calculate your time and expense before getting one of these. There were many models but they are all similar in design. These machines are very reliable and have cast iron frames (like the old cast iron sewing machines). They run very smooth and are still in use. Most parts are available new or used on eBay. The earliest models had few plastic parts but over the years they started to add more plastic parts, at first covers and doors, and then body panels. The earlier models have clockwise rotating hand-wheels (this is backwards from a newer machine). Most models do not have numbered tension knobs. Threading these machines is not overly difficult. Most of these machines use BLx1 needles. Max speed is 1500 SPM. Some of the models are as follows:

Juki MO-104 - 2/3 thread machine, M103 - 3 thread machine with numbered tension dials for needles and upper looper but lower looper dial is not numbered!

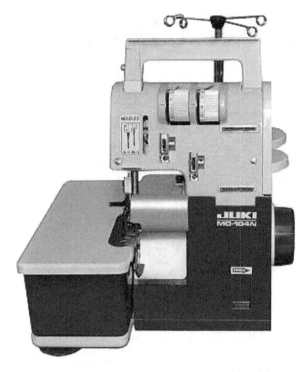

Juki MO-134 - 3/4 thread machine similar to the MO-104 shown above.

Baby Lock BL3-418 - 2/3 thread machine made by Juki.

Baby Lock BL4-605 - 3/4 thread machine made by Juki.

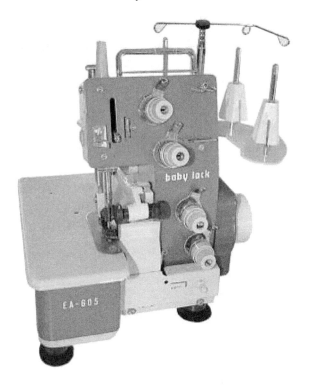

Industrial Machines

This chapter has general information about industrial overlock machines and gives an overview of some popular industrial overlock machine models that are now in production. The recommendations given in this chapter are my recommendations and opinions. Compare them with your requirements and decide what will work for you. I have no connection of any kind with the companies that make these machines. My criteria for recommending machines is value, reliability, ease of use and flexibility. The prices that are listed were at the time of writing of the book and may change.

Industrial sergers (usually called overlock machines) are built for continuous use in a production setting although they can also be used for small business or serious home use. Industrial sergers run at speeds of 4000 SPM to 9000 SPM depending on the model.

Industrial sergers are made for a specific range of stitch types, needle sizes, thread and fabrics. Make sure to get the right machine for the applications you need. There are many sub-models with special capabilities (Sub models are different versions of a model like 747A or 747B). Take your time and do your research!

Most industrial sergers can only make one stitch type. For this reason they are used primarily for high quantity production in a factory environment or for applications like hemming in an alteration shop that require the same stitch all the time. For product design work or small quantity work that requires a flexible machine that can make several stitch types a semi-pro (home) machine like the Juki MO-655 or MO-735 is preferable. The home machine is adjustable to a wide range of needle sizes and thread thicknesses. Most industrial machines can be converted from one sub-model configuration to another (such as from light to heavy materials) but this involves ordering parts that must be changed (feed dogs, loopers, needle plates, etc) and readjusting the machine with the new parts. This is expensive and time consuming.

Manufactures

Juki is the world leader in industrial overlock machines. I usually use them to compare other machines against. There are many other companies that make good industrial sergers of similar design such as Siruba, Pegasus, Brother, Rimoldi, Gemsy, Yamata (China Feiyue), etc. Siruba and Gemsy are now making direct drive machines with built in servo motors.

Service and parts - Check for service and parts availability in your country and city before you buy a machine. You can get parts and service for Juki almost anywhere in the world.

Tables and motors

Most industrial sergers are mounted in heavy tables and use large external motors mounted under the the table, although there are some new models that have direct drive servo motors built into the body of the machine. The external motors are the same as those used for industrial sewing machines. See the section "Motors" in the chapter "Industrial Machines" for complete information about motors.

Industrial sergers use recessed mountings in the table and can not use the same tables as industrial sewing machines. The tables have a hinged front section that lifts up for access to the lower parts of the machine for threading.

Lubrication systems

Industrial sergers have a lubrication system with an oil pump and oil reservoir. The lubrication system allows the machine to be used many hours a day at high speeds with little wear of the moving parts. When industrial sergers are shipped the oil must be drained and then replaced before the machine is used again. If the oil is not removed during shipment the oil may leak from the machine. Some models have oil free bearings or reduce oil bearings in the needle bar and the feed dog area to prevent oil contamination of the fabric going though the machine.

Needles

Most industrial overlock machines use the DCx27 needle system, some heavy-duty models use a DOx5 needle system. A standard duty machine will be set up for needles of about size 11 to 14. Heavy duty models are set up for size 16 or 18 needles and very heavy models are set up for size 21 or 23. Some industrial machines are set up for a certain application with a set needle size and require readjustment of the looper clearance to change needle size. Read the owners manual and specifications for your machine for recommended needle sizes to find out if adjustments are needed before you change needle sizes.

Features & Capabilities

Some of the features and capabilities that differ between models are as follows:

- **Stitches, threads and needles** - Most common are:
  - 3 thread (1 needle) type 504 Overlock stitch.
  - 4 thread (2 needle) type 514 Overlock stitch.
  - 5 thread (2 needle) type 516 Safety stitch (504 overlock + 401 chain stitch).
- **Needle gage** - This is the distance between the needles on two needle machines. For most machines it is between 2mm and 5mm. This is a set distance, it can not be changed so make sure that you get a machine with the needle gage that you need.
- **Easy to operate controls** - Some models are laid out with the controls in locations that make them easier to operate.
- **Differential Feed** - Most newer machines have differential feed. Differential feed uses separately adjustable feed dogs (one in front of the needle and the other behind the needle) to stretch or compress the fabric and prevent bunching or miss-feeding. This is a big advantage when sewing hard to handle fabrics such as knits or fabrics with slippery surfaces.
- **Top feed** - Some heavy-duty machines have upper feed claws that move similar to a walking foot

sewing machine. This is called "top feed", "upper and lower feed" or "tractor feed" depending on the manufacturer. Some models have two sets of top feed claws (front and back) to allow differential feed on both the top and bottom of the fabric.

- **Standard or heavy-duty** - Most models have both standard duty and heavy-duty sub-classes. The standard sub-classes are set up for small and medium sized needles and feed dogs with finer teeth. The heavy-duty sub-classes are set up for larger size needles, loopers with extra clearance, feed dogs with course teeth and possibly some other modifications like longer stitch lengths and higher foot clearance (standard foot clearance is 6mm or 7mm, heavy models have a foot clearance from 7mm to about 11mm.

- **Stitch length** - Most newer standard duty machines can vary the stitch length from .8mm to 4mm. Most heavy duty machines can vary the stitch length from 1.5mm to 5mm. Some models have a set stitch length that can not be changed.

- **Overlock Stitch width** - This is the width of the overlock portion of the stitch. For three and four thread machines this is the total stitch width. For safety stitch machines the needle gage is added to the overlock stitch width to the the total width of the safety stitch.

- **Double take up** - Some models have thread take up mechanisms for both the needle threads and looper threads for more even tension and allowing lighter tensions when desired.

- **Maximum Speed** - Industrial overlock machines have a maximum speed from 4000 SPM to 9000 SPM depending on the model. The actual top speed when in use is determined by the motor speed and the drive ratios of the pulleys. In most cases machines are set up so they run at less then the maximum speed. This is for increased reliability and to provide a safety margin for difficult conditions (thread or fabric problems, feed problems, etc).

- **Oil free needle bar** - Some models have oil free bearings on the needle bar to keep oil from getting on the fabric as it is being sewn.

- **Direct drive servo motor** - Some models now have motors that are built into the body of the machine. These machines have no drive belt. This reduces complexity and improves reliability. These machines are far more portable.

- **Cylinder bed** - Some machines have a cylinder bed (like a free arm on a home machine) that can be changed to a flat bed.

- **Auto chain cutter** - Cuts the chain automatically at the end of the seam.

- **Accessories** - Cut fabric collector bags, vacuum collectors, tape feeders, elastic feeders, auxiliary puller feed systems.

New machines

Because of modern manufacturing processes such as CNC machining the cost of many types of industrial machines have decreased over the last 20 years. Computer aided design has resulted in smoother running more reliable machines.

The following machines are the best value in their price range and are all good machines. If this is your first industrial machine check out the availability of parts and service in your location, or just get a Juki machine. Juki's may be slightly more expensive but they are serviced by just about all industrial service shops anywhere in the world.

Make sure that you match the machine to your needs. Industrial sergers are not as generalized as home sergers, they are set up for a more specific range of stitch types and materials. If you need to sew heavy fabric make sure to get a machine that is set up for heavy fabric and make sure that the machine can accept the needle sizes you need and can make the stitch types you need. Some industrial sergers can only make one stitch type and are set up for one weight of fabric. Take your time and do your research!

Gemsy GEM737F, GEM747F, GEM757F ($599 ot $699 on-line sellers) - These standard workhorse 3, 4 and 5 thread models come in a wide range of submodels. "H" models are heavy duty with size 18 needles. Check for availability of parts and service in your country. Gemsy makes a large range of other models as well.

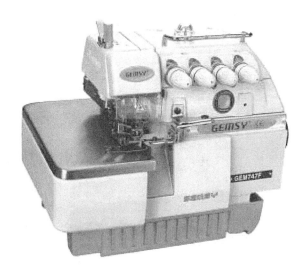

Yamata (China Feiyue) FY737A, FY747A, FY757A and similar models ($780 eBay sellers) - These standard workhorse 3, 4 and 5 thread models come in a wide range of submodels. Availability of parts is good in the US because Yamata has an office and distribution center in Florida, check for availability of parts and service in your country. Yamata makes a large range of other models as well.

Siruba 700K series (737, 747, 757 and similar models) ($850 on-line sellers) - These standard workhorse 3, 4 and 5 thread models come in a wide range of submodels. "UX" submodels are heavy duty. Availability of parts is good in the US because Siruba is distributed by several large industrial dealers, check for availability of parts and service in your country. Siruba makes a large range of other models as well.

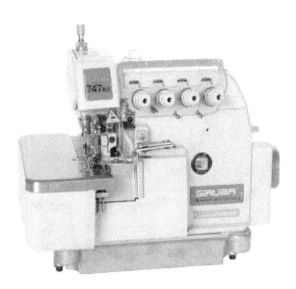

Siruba 700Q series Direct drive ($1295 eBay sellers) - These machines have built in servo motors and the motor electronics are also built into the body of the machine. This results in energy efficiency and the machine is more portable. 3, 4, 5 and 6 thread models come in a wide range of submodels.

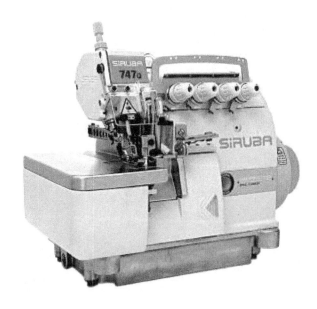

Juki MO-6700 series (6714S $1487 Amazon) - These standard workhorse 3, 4 and 5 thread models come in a wide range of submodels. "H" submodels are heavy duty. A wide range of attachments are available for these machines. "6700D models are semi-dry head machines (needle bar and upper looper do not use oil).

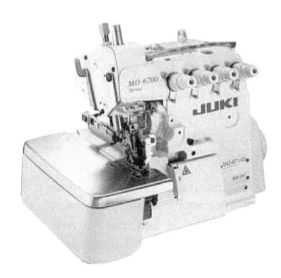

Juki MO-6900 series (6916S $1750 Amazon) - High speed models (8000 SPM) with improved tension systems. There are 3, 4 and 5 thread models that come in a wide range of submodels. "H" submodels are heavy duty. A wide range of attachments are available for these machines. "J" models are for extra heavy materials and have tractor feed "C" models are cylinder bed.

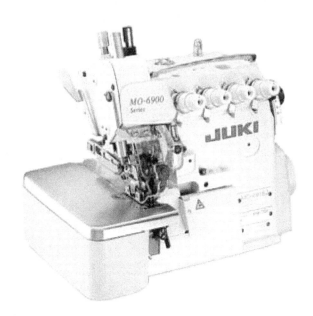

Merrow Machine - This is one of the only surviving US based sewing machine companies. They make many types of overlock machines and they will make custom machines for your specific application (even if you only need a single machine). Check out their web site to get more info about their models.

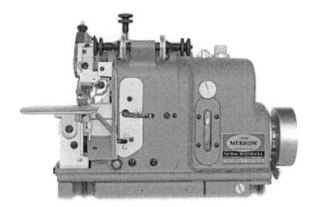

- **The MG-3 series** models are hemming machines and make a 3 thread overlock stitch type 504. They can also be used for many decorative applications and make the classic merrowed edge.
- **The MG-4 series** models are 2/3 thread and make a type 514 stitch. The MG-4FO makes an improved flatlock type stitch for active-ware and other applications.
- **The 70, 71 and 72 series** models make the butt seam stitch type 501. Some models of these machines are very heavy-duty and can sew carpet and other thick materials.
- **The 18 series** models make a single thread crochet stitch.

Used Machines

In general there is little reason to buy a used industrial overlock machine unless it is fully tested, running perfectly and is being offered at a very low price. The reason is that very good new machines are now available for under $1000. Because most industrial overlock machines are specialized for a specific type of work it is unlikely that a used machine is of the correct subclass for the type of work that you need. Be sure to check used machines for leaking oil seals around the needle bar, loopers and feed dog area.

Coverstitch Machines

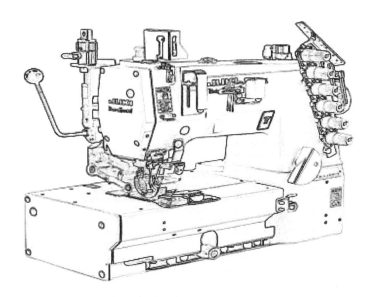

Coverstitch machines make the coverstitch and come in both home and industrial versions. We will go over some home coverstitch machines in this chapter. Some sergers can also make the coverstitch such as the Singer 14T968DC and Juki MO-735. Industrial coverstitch machines cost about $1500 and up. They are available in many configurations from most of the same manufacturers that make industrial overlock machines. Juki is a good starting place if you are looking for an industrial coverstitch machine.

Coverstitches are used primarily in garment construction for flat seaming. The coverstitch is often used for finishing (decoration) as a final operation but can also be used for seaming and finishing in one operation. In the picture below a single face three needle coverstitch is shown, as you can see one side of the fabric has the coverstitch facing but the other side looks like three straight chain stitches running in parallel. Some machines can make a double face coverstitch with the facing on both sides of the fabric.

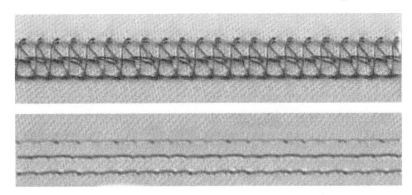

- Three thread single face cover stitches are made with two needle threads and one looper thread. They are used to cover the folded edges of fabric or folded seams.
- Four thread single face cover stitches are made with three needle threads and one looper thread. They are used in garment construction and form a decorative and functional stitch that will cover folded seams.

Home Coverstitch Machines

Brother 2340CV ($387 on Amazon) - This machine looks just like a serger but makes cover stitches. This is a 3 needle, 1 looper machine and makes the 4 thread single face cover stitch. It can also make a 3 thread cover stitch by using 2 needles and a 2 thread chain stitch by using only one needle. Max speed is 1000 SPM. Features include differential feed, stitch length 2mm to 4mm, stitch width 3mm or 6mm, right hand side presser foot lift lever, Color coded threading, adjustable presser foot pressure.

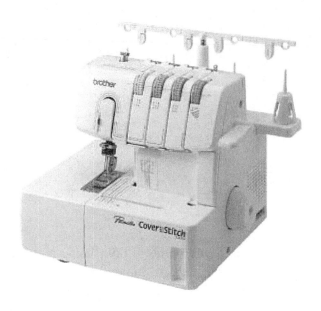

Janome CoverPro 900CPX ($399 on Amazon) - This is a 2 needle, 1 looper machine and makes the 3 thread single face cover stitch. Janome also makes a 3 needle model, the CoverPro 1000CPX.

Singer 14T968DC ($419 on Amazon) - 2/3/4/5 thread serger, that can also make the 2 and 3 needle coverstitch and 2 thread chain stitch. This machine has a lot of capabilities for the price! If you are technically proficient you will have no problem, but if not the learning curve for this machine may be a problem for you. Has good documentation and workbooks available on the Singer web site.

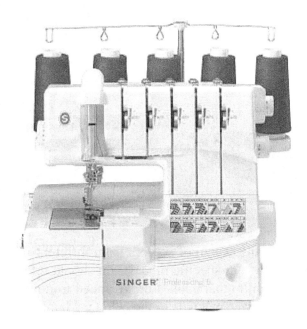

Juki MO-735 ($899 on-line dealers) - This is a 2/3/4/5 thread serger that will also make a 2 and 3 needle cover stitch and a 2 thread chain stitch. Max speed is 1500 SPM, Differential feed, stitch length 1mm to 4mm, stitch width 2mm for rolled hem, 5mm to 7mm overlock stitches and 10mm for the chain and safety stitches, color coded threading, adjustable presser foot pressure. Juki makes high quality machines, all of their models are very good. Uses regular home type needles (130/705 H).

Troubleshooting

There is a great deal of variation in the design of sergers from different manufactures so the information in this book may not apply exactly to your specific model, you should refer to the owners manual for your specific model of machine in addition to this book. For advanced troubleshooting you may need to get a service manual (see the section on service manuals in the chapter Maintenance & Repair).

NOTE: Always troubleshoot your machine with regular serger thread and set the tensions to the normal settings that are specified in your owners manual. Make sure that you are using the correct needle as specified by your owners manual. For most machines it is best to use a size 14 needle for troubleshooting. Set your serger to a medium stitch length and medium stitch width. Your machine was adjusted this way from the factory and should function properly with these settings. Test your machine with 2 layers of medium weight cotton material (like an old bed sheet or pillow case).

Use the section **Troubleshooting By Symptom** if your machine is in good condition and you want to track down a single problem (for instance if your machine is breaking the needle or has tension problems). The Troubleshooting By Symptom section is a quicker checklist and does not go as deep as the In-depth Diagnostic checklist does.

Use the **In-depth Diagnostic** to do a complete check if you are having serious problems or multiple problems. You can also use this list for maintenance or if you get a used machine and want do a complete check of the machine.

Troubleshooting by symptom

Thread breaks or stitch not forming correctly

- **Check the threading** - Is the machine threaded correctly? Un-thread and carefully re-thread the machine to be absolutely sure that the machine is threaded correctly. Take your time. Do you have a threading diagram? Most machines have a threading diagram printed on the inside of the looper cover or other location. All machines have a threading diagram in the owners manual. Sometimes threading a serger is not intuitive and it is possible (even for someone experienced) to miss-thread the machine. Miss-threading is the #1 cause of problems. You need to eliminate this as a possibility.

- **Check the needle** - Is the needle OK and not dull or bent? Is the needle inserted all the way into the needle bar before being tightened? Try a new needle (or needles) and make sure it is inserted properly. Be sure the needle is the correct size and type. Too small a needle can cause tension problems and thread breakage. Check your user manual to find out what type and size of needle you should be using for your machine. Check that the thread is not too thick for the size of needle you are using. Most machines ship with a size 14 needle from the factory and that is a good size for all general purpose serging.
- **Problems with thick seams?**
    - Make sure that you are not pushing or pulling the fabric through the machine, the feed dogs must do the work. See the section "Serger Operation" in the chapter "Threading & Basic Use".
    - Check the presser foot pressure, it may need to be increased. If there is insufficient presser foot presser the fabric will not feed correctly while sewing a thick seam. If the fabric feeds incorrectly or stops feeding it will cause the stitches to form in the same spot and the stitches will pile up on the stitch finger. This may cause the needle to bend or break.
- **Check the thread** - Check to make sure that the thread does not have knots, tangles or is sticking on the cone or spool. Does the thread un-roll from the cone smoothly? Check that the thread is not caught on the thread cone and that the thread is not sticking or tangled in the thread tree and guides. Check for bad or rotted thread. Try breaking some of the thread in your hands, is it as strong as it should be? Compare to other thread if you are not sure. Some thread rots when it gets old and some thread is bad from the manufacturer, so never rule out bad thread.
- **Are the tension disks and thread path OK?** - First double check to see if the tension knobs are set to the recommended setting for your machine (specified in your owners manual).
    - To test the tension disks and thread path for the needle threads cut the thread at the needle (or needles) and pull some thread out from the thread guides on the needle bar (closest to the needles). Pull the thread for each needle individually (one at a time). Pay attention to the way it feels as you are pulling the thread. Does one of the threads pull different than the other? (If you have a one needle machine then compare to the looper threads.) Do the threads pull smoothly but with some tension? If one of the threads pulls without tension or with too much tension then that thread has a problem.
    - To test the tension disks and thread path for the looper threads cut the threads after the loopers and pull some thread out from each looper. Pull the thread for each looper individually (one at a time). Pay attention to the way it feels as you are pulling the thread. Does one of the threads pull different than the other? Do the threads pull smoothly but with some tension? If one of the threads pulls without tension or with too much tension then that thread has a problem.
    - If a thread pulls too easily then the thread may not be seated correctly in the tension disks or slot or there may be lint or old thread stuck in the disks (preventing the disks from providing tension).
    - If a thread pulls with too much difficulty then find out where it is stuck or sticking. Is the tension adjustment too tight or malfunctioning? Is the thread tangled in a thread guide or around some other part?
    - If you can't resolve the problem then you probably need to disassemble and repair the offending tension disk assembly (or have it repaired).
    - Are you using too high a thread tension for the size of thread you are using? Too high a thread tension can break light weight thread or cause the machine to stitch erratically.
- **Is the fabric feeding correctly?** - Are the feed dogs moving the fabric properly through the machine? Is the fabric moving forward? Check and adjust the presser foot pressure if your machine has adjustable presser foot pressure, it will explain how to do this in your owners manual. Try a long stitch length to make sure the fabric is moving through the machine. If the fabric is not moving try testing the machine with no thread and see if the fabric is moving. Also go to the next

step and check the cutting knives to make sure that they are working correctly and not obstructing the fabric from moving through the machine. Check that the stitch length is not too short, this can cause the machine to jam with thick thread or certain fabrics.

- **Are the cutting knives OK?** - (for machines with a cutter). If the cutters are dull or miss-aligned they can cause the machine not to feed correctly. Test the cutters with no thread in the machine. Are the cutters cutting smoothly and making a nice clean cut? Try 2 or three layers of material. If the cutters work with no thread and the fabric feeds properly and is cut cleanly then the cutters should work when the machine is threaded.
- **Needle hole area OK?** - Check to see that a needle did not hit and damage the needle plate and the around the needle hole or slot.
- **Still not working?** - If none of the above checks isolate the problem then you may want to go through the complete In-depth diagnostic or take your machine to a service shop.

Needle breakage

- **Check the needles** - Check that your needles OK and not bent or defective. Inspect the needle or needles (see the section "Inspecting needles" in chapter "Needles" or try a new needle. You can also try a needle from another manufacturer to make sure that you did not get a bad batch of needles.
- **Is the needle inserted properly?** - Is it all the way into the needle bar before being tightened? Is the needle clamp or needle screw tight?
- **Is it the correct needle?** - Is the needle the correct size and from the correct needle system? (see the chapter Needles). Is the needle size too small for the fabric thickness or for sewing through thick seams? Most sergers come from the factory with a size 14 needle installed.
- **Problems with thick fabric or seams?** - Does the needle break when sewing thick fabric or thick seams? Is the fabric feeding through the machine correctly on thick seams? Make sure that you are not pushing or pulling the fabric through the machine, the feed dogs have to do the work. If you push or pull the fabric it will bend the needle and the needle will hit the needle plate and break instead of going through the needle hole. The feed dogs move the fabric only when the needle is up they do not move the fabric when the needle is down so they will not bend the needle. If you pull the fabric through the machine you will bend or break the needle. See the chapter "Threading & Basic Use" for more about serger operation.
- **Are the feed dogs working?** - Are the feed dogs moving the fabric through the machine properly? Is the fabric moving forward? Try a long stitch length to make sure the fabric is moving through the machine. If the stitch is too short or if the fabric is not moving then the machine will stitch in the same place many times and make a thread knot that will break the needle. If the fabric is not moving try the machine with no thread and see if the fabric is moving. If the fabric is not moving though the machine then the machine has a feed problem that needs to be fixed, or the cutter is jammed (see the chapter Maintenance & Repair).
- **Are the cutting knives OK?** - (for machines with a cutter). If the cutters are dull or miss-aligned they can cause the machine to not feed correctly. Test the cutters with no thread in the machine. Are the cutters cutting smoothly and making a nice clean cut? Try 2 or three layers of material. If the cutters work with no thread and the fabric feeds properly and cuts cleanly then the machine will usually work with thread. If the fabric is jamming at the cutters then the cutters will need to be adjusted or replaced. See your owners manual for instructions on replacing the cutters for your model of machine.

Fabric bunching or waiving

- With thin fabrics the stitch length may be too long with high needle tension. Try reducing the needle thread tension or go to a shorter stitch length.

- If your machine has differential feed then try various settings to see if you can get the fabric to feed correctly and eliminate the bunching or waiving.

Machine runs slow or is noisy

- Oil the machine. Most machines need regular lubrication. See your owners manual for oiling instructions for your specific model of machine. For more on oiling see the chapter "Maintenance & Repair".
- Check for tangled up thread in any of the mechanical parts of the machine.
- Go through the Machine Checklist later in this chapter.

Machine does not run

- If the motor runs but the hand wheel does not turn then the machine has a loose or broken drive belt..See the chapter on "Maintenance & Repair" or take your machine to a service shop.
- If the motor makes a humming or buzzing sound but does not run then the motor or the machine is frozen or jammed. See the chapter on "Maintenance & Repair" or take your machine to a service shop.
- If the machine makes no sound or has no power make sure that the foot pedal is plugged in to the machine. Check to make sure that the machine is getting power and is plugged in to an active wall outlet. If you are able to obtain the use of another foot pedal and power cord (must be the correct model) you should try that with your machine, then you will know if the problem is in the foot pedal and power cord or in the machine. If that does not fix the problem see the chapter on "Maintenance & Repair" or take your machine to a service shop.

In-depth diagnostic

Thread path checklist

Thread path problems are by far the most frequently encountered problems with sergers and overlock machines. Being able to quickly troubleshoot thread path problems will make for a much happier sewing experience and increase your confidence in your serger. It is a good idea to periodically check the thread path even when there is no problem, you can do a short version of the checklist while you are threading the machine. Over a period of time you will increase the speed that you go though the checklist until it becomes second nature.

If going through the thread path checklist fails to solve your problem then you should continue to the looper checklist and the machine checklist. With experience you can jump into the appropriate checklist at the place where you think the problem will be found instead of going through the entire checklist each time.

The clearances that are listed in this book are for a general range of machines but may not be correct for your exact model of machine. If you have access to a service manual for your machine you should use the procedures and clearances in the service manual but for some older machines it is not possible to obtain a service manual and in that case the clearances listed in this book will probably work.

First run through the checklist and make sure the machine works correctly with general purpose polyester serger thread (or the thread you normally use in the case of industrial machines). Use a new medium size needle. For home sergers this would be a size 14 needle. For industrial machines use the needle size you normally use with your machine. After you have the machine working correctly with general purpose thread and standard size needles then change to a different thread and needle if needed and run through the checklist again. For testing use a medium stitch length and medium stitch width.

- **Clean the machine** - Clean the thread path and check that there is no lint or pieces of old thread stuck in the thread path. The thread path is everywhere the thread goes through when the machine is threaded. Make sure the looper area and feed dog area are free from old thread or scraps of cloth.
- **Thread cones** - The thread must leave the cones smoothly or there will be tension problems. To test the cone, mount the thread cone on the machine and pass the thread through the fist thread guide on the top of the thread tree. Grab the end of the thread after the first guide and slowly pull out a few feet of thread from the cone. Did the thread pull smoothly with little or no tension? If not you have to find out why and fix the problem. Some old thread cones are miss-wound or have sticking thread for some reason.
- **Correct threading** - Make absolutely sure that your machine is threaded correctly. Try pulling out all thread and re-threading the machine. Most sergers have a threading diagram on the inside of the looper cover and in the owners manual. Follow the threading diagram for your machine. If you can't get a owners manual then look on the Internet to see if you can find a threading diagram for your machine. If your not sure then take your machine to a repair shop and have a sewing machine mechanic show you how to thread the machine properly.
- **Thread guides** - Make sure that the thread pulls smoothly through all thread guides. Use a thick thread such a button thread to clean the thread guides like you would use dental floss to clean your teeth. The inner surface of thread guides can get crudded up with lint or rust that you can't see and this can cause the thread to catch.
- **Test the tension disks** - Thread the machine except do not thread the needle (needles) or loopers. Set the thread tension to zero. Grab the end of the thread after it goes through the thread guide after the tension disks and pull out a few feet of thread. The thread should pull out smoothly with little resistance. Do this for each thread. Now set the tensions to 1 and pull out more thread. The thread should be harder to pull but should still pull out smoothly. Try it at 2, 3, 4 and 5. If your machine does not have numbers on the tension adjustment dials then just imagine a range from 1 to 10 and set the dial accordingly. As you increase the tension it should be harder to pull the thread but the thread should pull smoothly. If the thread sticks or does not pull smoothly then you need to clean the tension disks as follows:
    - Use a length of white button thread or other thick thread and slide it back and forth through the tension disks to clean them (like using dental floss on your teeth). White color button thread allows you to see any lint, dirt or rust that comes out. It is a good idea to periodically clean the tension disks in this manner. If this does not solve the problem then the tension disks need to be dis-assembled and inspected. You may be able to do this yourself (see the chapter "Maintenance & Repair") or you can take the machine to a service shop.
- **Needle** - Replace the needle with a new one. This is to eliminate the possibility of a bent needle. Even a slightly bent needle can cause problems. Check to see that the needle is seated correctly and that the needle clamp or screw is tight. Is the needle scarf facing the back of the machine? On most sergers the needle scarf should face the back of the machine. See the chapter "Needles" for a description of the needle scarf.
- **Test sew** - Re-thread the machine and test sew. It is best to use fabric that is the opposite color from the thread so that you can clearly see the stitching. Is the stitch forming correctly now? If not then proceed with the looper and needle checklist next.

Looper and needle checklist

First we will do some preliminary things:

- **Looper and feed dog area cleaning** - Use a small brush and Q-tips (and a vacuum cleaner if one is handy) to remove all lint and thread from the looper and feed dog area.
- **Lubrication** - Look in the owners manual for your machine and see if your machine requires oiling. If required then oil the looper shaft bearings and other parts that your owners manual specifies.
- **Check the looper tips for damage** - Inspect the points of the upper and lower loopers by feel or by using a magnifier or magnifying glasses. The looper tips should be sharp and the rest of the looper should have a smooth surface and should not have burrs, scratches or damage from wear. If the tips are damaged or have burs the looper must be replaced.

Now we will check the critical alignments of the machine starting with the needle bar height and lower looper timing. Each of these alignments must be correct for the machine to correctly form a stitch.

Needle bar height

Turn the hand-wheel slowly in the direction of normal rotation until the needle is in the lowest position. The tip of the lower looper should be about 3mm to 7mm from the shaft of the needle as shown in the picture below. If this is not the case then go to the chapter Adjustments and see the section on adjusting the lower looper timing or take your machine to a service shop.

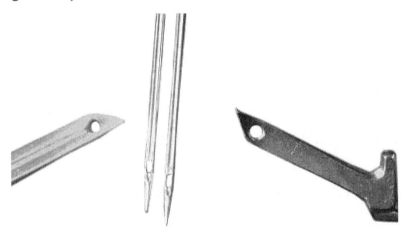

Continue to turn the handwheel in the direction of normal rotation until the tip of the lower looper is at the needle. This is shown in the picture below. The tip of the lower looper should be in the middle area of the scarf of the needle. If this is not the case then the needle bar height will need to be adjusted, go the the chapter Adjustments and see the section on adjusting the needle bar height or take your machine to a service shop.

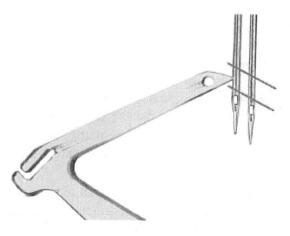

In the picture above the scarf of the needle is facing to the back so you can't see it in the picture. The lower looper in the picture will pass by the back side of the needle and will pass through the scarf area. The scarf can be seen in the picture of the needle below. The scarf is a flattened part of the needle specifically made to allow the lower looper to pass by without hitting the needle. If the needle bar height is wrong the lower looper will try to pass by the needle too high or too low and hit the shaft or eye of the needle. The main reason for the needle bar height to come out of adjustment is the needle hitting the needle plate while the machine is running.

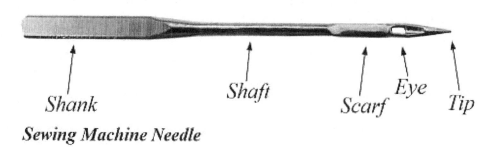

Shank   Shaft   Scarf   Eye   Tip

Sewing Machine Needle

Lower looper to needle clearance

Turn the hand-wheel in the normal direction of rotation until the needle has reached its lowest point and then slowly continue to turn the handwheel until the tip of the lower looper is has crossed to center of the needle. This is shown on the left side of the picture below. Look at the clearance between the tip of the lower looper and the scarf of the needle. For machines with two needles we are talking about the left hand needle.

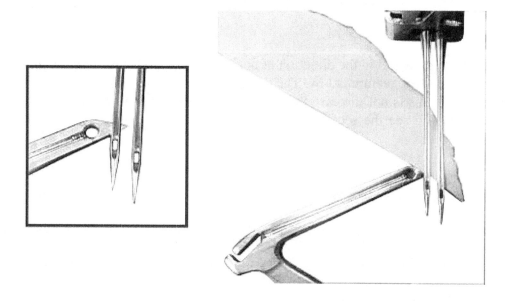

- **Optimal Clearance** - You should be able to pass a piece of copy machine paper between the needle and the looper (about .1mm of clearance).
- **Insufficient Clearance** - The needle should not actually touch the looper. If it looks like the needle is touching the looper then rock the hand-wheel back and forth slightly and watch the needle very closely as the tip of the looper comes across the scarf of the needle. Is the tip of the lower looper contacting the needle and pushing it out of the way? Can you see the needle bend slightly as the tip of the lower looper goes by? If this is the case there is insufficient clearance. What we want is for the tip of the lower looper to come very close to the scarf of the needle (about .1mm or the distance of a piece of copy machine paper), but we do not want the tip of the looper to actually touch the needle. If the tip of the looper touches the needle it will need to be adjusted. See the section Lower looper to needle clearance in the chapter Adjustments
- **Excessive Clearance** - If the tip of the lower looper is more than .3mm away from the scarf of the needle (two or three pieces of paper). This is too much clearance and can cause missed stitches, the looper will need to be adjusted. See the section Lower looper to needle clearance in the chapter Adjustments or take your machine to a service shop

Lower looper timing

Lower looper timing - With the needle in its lowest position the lower looper should be at or close to its left-most position. The tip of the lower looper should be to the left of the needle by 3mm to 7mm on most machines. For machines with two needles we are talking about the left hand needle. This is shown in the picture below, the lower looper is on the left.

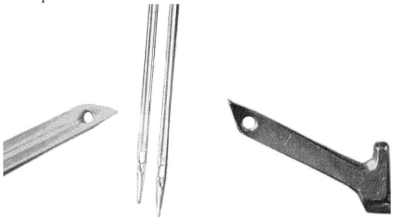

As the hand-wheel is slowly turned in the normal direction of rotation the needle will rise and the tip of the lower looper will move towards the needle. Stop turning when the tip of the lower looper has reached the needle. At this point the needle should have raised about 3mm from its lowest position. The tip of the lower looper should be in the central area of the scarf of the needle as shown in the picture below. The tip of the lower looper must go through the scarf of the needle to catch the needle thread or the stitch will not form correctly.

If the tip of the lower looper is not going through the scarf area of the needle the lower looper timing will need adjustment, see the chapter Adjustments or take your machine to a service shop.

Upper looper to lower looper clearance - Start with the needle in the lowest position and slowly turn the handwheel in the normal direction of rotation until the tip of the upper looper is just passing by the lower looper. This is shown in the picture below on the left. The clearance between the tip of the upper looper and the lower looper should be more than .1mm (or one piece of copy machine paper). The tip of the upper looper should not touch the lower looper at any point. In the picture below on the right you can see that the tip of the upper looper is catching the thread from the lower looper. The tip of the upper looper must be close enough to the lower looper to reliably catch the thread, if it is too far away it will not catch the thread. If the upper looper to lower looper clearance looks wrong see the chapter Adjustments or take your machine to a service shop.

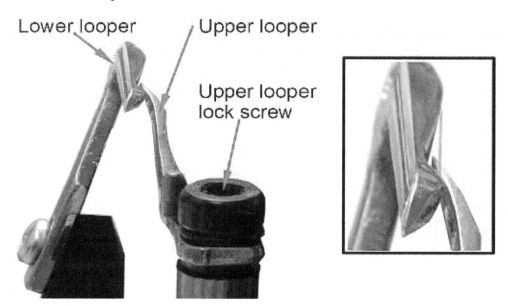

Upper looper to needle clearance - Start with the needle in the highest position. Turn the hand-wheel in the normal direction of rotation until the tip of the needle (or needles) is half way across the scarf of the upper looper. Check the clearance between the tip of the needle (or needles) and the scarf of the upper looper. The clearance should be more than .1mm (one piece of copy machine paper). The picture below shows the clearance being checked.

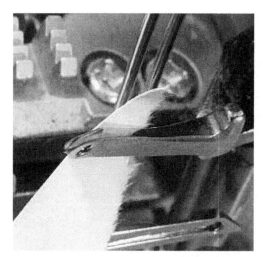

The upper looper must be close enough to the needle so that the needle can catch the thread from the upper looper as it moves down toward the fabric. This is shown in the picture below, you can see the needles catching the green thread from the upper looper. To summarize the upper looper should not touch the needle but be close enough so that the needle can catch the upper looper thread. If this is not the case see the chapter Adjustments or take your machine to a service shop.

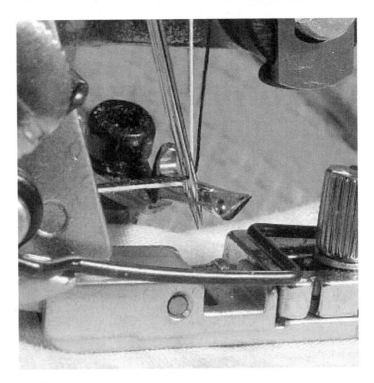

Cutting blade checklist

- If the blades are not cutting the fabric correctly the fabric will not feed through the machine correctly and this can cause the machine to stitch many times in the same place on the fabric, this will eventually jam the machine.
- Check to make sure that the mounting screws for the blades are not loose. If they are loose then tighten them. Also check to see that the blades are adjusted correctly (if they are adjustable, not all blades are adjustable), the owners manual for your machine should tell how to do this.
- When the blades become worn and no longer cut the fabric cleanly then replace one or both blades as needed. One of the cutting blades (usually the upper blade) is made of a very hard steel and does not need replacing very often, the other blade (usually the lower blade) is made of a softer type of steel and will need to be replaced more often. Most new machines come with at least one replacement blade, otherwise they can be ordered from the manufacturer or most on-line suppliers.

Machine checklist

- Does the motor run? - Does the hand wheel turn? If the machine will not run but the motor makes a buzzing sound then the motor or the machine is frozen. If this is the case go to the chapter Maintenance & Repair.
- Machine going slow? The machine may need oiling or there may be grease in places where oil should be. Another cause may be that someone oiled the machine with the wrong type of oil. See the chapter Maintenance & Repair.
- Noise and smoothness test - With the presser foot in the up position and no thread in the machine, run the machine at various speeds and listen for anything wrong. The machine should sound smooth. If you are not sure if the machine sounds OK then go to where you can hear a similar machine to learn what you should be hearing. Sometimes you can see videos of machines running on YouTube. If the machine seams slow and sluggish it may need to be lubricated. If you hear any clicking sounds or anything that sounds like metal parts hitting each other this is a problem. Go to the chapter Maintenance & Repair.

Test sewing

Test sew on a piece of scrap fabric and inspect the stitches. To test a machine for correct operation it is best to use opposite colors of thread and fabric so that the stitches are clearly visible.

Adjustments

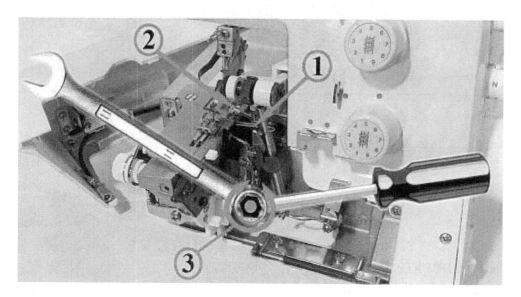

PLEASE READ FIRST -This chapter covers the basics of serger adjustment and was written with a generic machine in mind. Sergers differ greatly from model to model. The procedures in this chapter may not exactly apply to your machine, but are presented to give you general understanding of how the adjustments are done and why. **If at all possible you should get a service manual for your specific model of machine.** Use your better judgment and if any part of the procedures do not seem appropriate for your machine you should stop and obtain a service manual (see the section on service manuals in the chapter "Maintenance & Repair".

The if you are doing more than one adjustment or are working with a machine that has multiple issues you should do the adjustments in the order they are presented below, this is important because some of the earlier adjustments will have an effect on the adjustments presented further in the chapter.

Industrial machines with curved needles - The following procedures are for machines with straight needles. If you have an industrial machine with curved needles such as a Merrow Machine or old Singer overlock machine the procedures in this book probably will not work well, you will need to get a service manual. Both Merrow and Singer make some of their manuals available on line for free download.

Preparation

- Un-plug the machine.
- Un-thread the machine.
- Remove the presser foot.
- In the procedures below only turn the hand-wheel by hand (not using the motor because the machine should be unplugged).
- Replace the needle in the machine with a new name-brand needle (Organ, Schmetz, Singer, etc) before doing adjustments to the machine. If you adjust the machine to a bent or bad quality needle some of the adjustments will be wrong. Check your needles to make sure they are straight because even new needles have some variation, they are not all perfectly straight. You should check a few needles for straightness and use the straightest needle, lets say you have five needles you will find that three of them are probably about the same and the other two may vary slightly. If they are all

very different you should discard them and buy new needles, but lets say that at least 3 of them are very close, then use one of these needles to adjust the machine. The chapter "Needles" explains how to check if a needle is straight.

• Have a set of high power reading glasses handy (to use as a magnifier) or a magnifying glass. A bright light that is direct-able or a flashlight is also handy.

Needle bar height

Turn the handwheel of the machine until the needle is in its highest position. If you have a service manual for your machine it should give you a measurement between the tip of the needle and the top surface of the needle plate. The picture below on the right side shows this measurement. To make the adjustment loosen the needle bar lock screw or nut, position the needle bar to the correct height and re-tighten the lock screw or nut. This is shown in the picture on the left. You may have to slightly rotate the needle bar to get it to move. When it is set to the correct height make sure that the needle is facing forward before tightening the lock screw and is not rotated to one side. Make sure that the needle is at its highest position and recheck the measurement. This method is the best way to adjust the needle bar height. If you do not have a service manual you can measure the needle bar height of another good running machine that is the exact same model as your machine if you can find one.

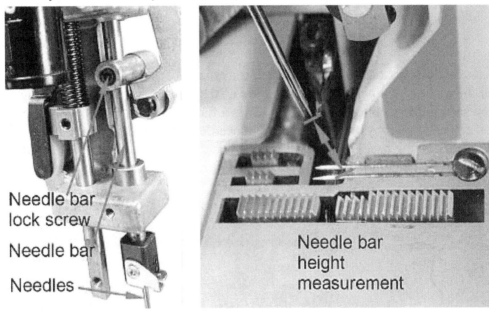

Needle bar lock screw

Needle bar

Needles

Needle bar height measurement

If you do not have a service manual and do not have access to another machine to measure you can try to adjust the needle bar height by a second method as follows but this is not the preferred method. Turn the hand-wheel slowly in the direction of normal rotation until the needle is in the lowest position. The tip of the lower looper should be about 5mm to 7mm from the shaft of the needle as shown in the picture below. If this is not the case then first adjust the lower looper timing.

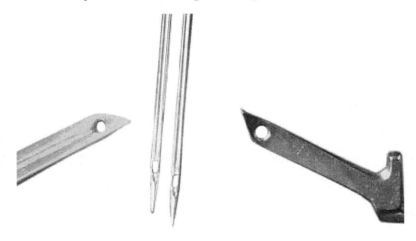

Continue to turn the handwheel in the direction of normal rotation until the tip of the lower looper is at the needle. This is shown in the picture below. The tip of the lower looper should be in the middle area of the scarf of the needle. If this is not the case then the needle bar height will need to be adjusted. To make the adjustment loosen the needle bar lock screw or nut, position the needle bar to the correct height and re-tighten the lock screw or nut. You may have to rotate the needle bar to get it to move. When it is set to the correct height make sure that the needle is facing forward before tightening the lock screw and is not rotated to one side. Rotate the handwheel one turn until the tip of the lower looper is at the needle and recheck the measurement.

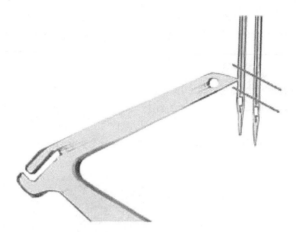

In the picture above the scarf of the needle is facing to the back so you can't see it in the picture. The lower looper in the picture will pass by the back side of the needle and will pass through the scarf area. The scarf can be seen in the picture below. The scarf is a flattened part of the needle specifically made to allow the lower looper to pass by without hitting the needle. If the needle bar height is wrong the lower looper will try to pass by the needle too high or too low and hit the shaft or eye of the needle. The main reason for the needle bar height to come out of adjustment is the needle hitting the needle plate while the machine is running.

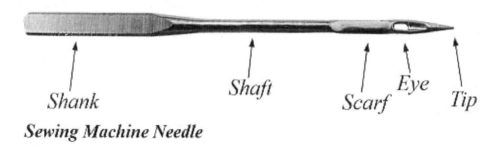

Shank   *Shaft*   *Scarf*   *Eye*   *Tip*

Sewing Machine Needle

Needle deflectors

Most machines have needle deflectors. The needle deflectors are active in the area of the lower looper and are there to guide (deflect) the needle into a straight line of travel if the needle is getting pushed by the fabric.

Front needle deflector

Some machines have a front side needle deflector. This deflector is mounted to the needle plate or to the frame of the machine. If your machine does not have a front needle deflector then skip this adjustment. The needle defector is not supposed to have contact with the needle during normal operation (or minimal contact only) and is there in case the fabric causes the needle to bend. If the fabric pushes the needle and tries to bend it, the job of the front needle deflector is to prevent the needle from bending away from the looper which would cause skipped stitches.

- Turn the hand-wheel in the normal direction of rotation and watch the tip of the needle and it moves down to the lowest point in its travel. Look closely to see if if there is a front needle deflector, it will be to the front of the needle (and the lower looper will be at the back side of the needle). If you see a deflector then watch as the needle passes the defector. The needle should pass close to the defector (about .1mm or the thickness of a piece of copy machine paper). The needle may touch the defector but the defector should not cause the needle to bend.

- If the front side deflector clearance is insufficient (causing the needle to bend) or excessive (more than .3mm) then you will need to adjust it. Most needle defectors have a simple screw that allows them to be loosened for adjustment. Loosen the adjustment screw and move the defector so that the clearance is correct and then re-tighten the screw. Recheck the clearance after you do this.

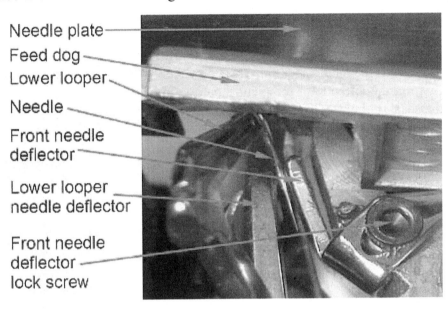

Needle plate
Feed dog
Lower looper
Needle
Front needle deflector
Lower looper needle deflector
Front needle deflector lock screw

Lower looper needle deflector

Some machines have a lower looper needle deflector. This deflector is mounted to the lower looper drive arm. If your machine does not have a lower looper needle deflector then skip this step. The lower looper needle defector is not supposed to have contact with the needle during normal operation or only very light contact. It is there in case the fabric causes the needle to deflect (bend) to the back of the machine. If the needle bends the job of the lower looper needle deflector is to prevent the needle from hitting the tip of the lower looper which could cause the lower looper to hit the needle and possibly severely bend the needle and damage the lower looper.

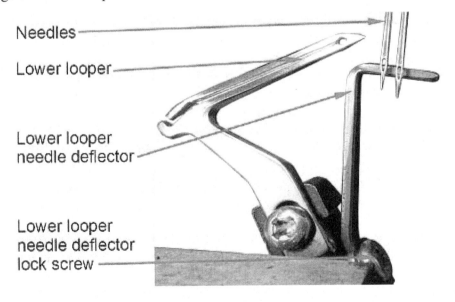

Needles
Lower looper
Lower looper needle deflector
Lower looper needle deflector lock screw

- To adjust the lower looper needle deflector rotate the handwheel until the needle is in the area of the lower looper needle deflector as pictured above. Check the clearance between the deflector and the needle as the deflector moves by the needle. The deflector should be just touching the needle or very close to touching the needle but should not cause the needle to bend. You have to look very closely to see if the needle is bending or not. If the deflector clearance is not correct then adjust it. Some machines have an adjustment screw that can simply be turned to adjust the clearance. Some machines (like in the picture above) have a lock screw that must be loosened, the deflector moved to the correct position and the lock screw re-tightend. After you adjust the clearance, re-check it after rotating the handwheel one turn.

Lower looper to needle clearance

Turn the hand-wheel in the normal direction of rotation until the needle has reached its lowest point and then slowly continue to turn the handwheel until the tip of the lower looper is has crossed to center of the needle. This is shown on the left side of the picture below. Look at the clearance between the tip of the lower looper and the scarf of the needle. For machines with two needles we are talking about the left hand needle.

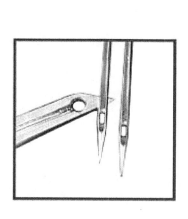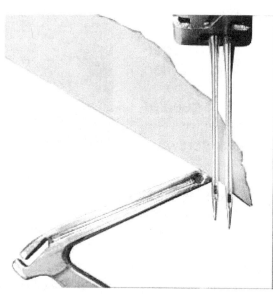

- **Optimal Clearance** - You should be able to pass a piece of copy machine paper between the needle and the looper (about .1mm of clearance).
- **Insufficient Clearance** - The needle should not actually touch the looper. If it looks like the needle is touching the looper then rock the hand-wheel back and forth slightly and watch the needle very closely as the tip of the looper comes across the scarf of the needle. Is the tip of the lower looper contacting the needle and pushing it out of the way? Can you see the needle bend slightly as the tip of the lower looper goes by? If this is the case there is insufficient clearance. What we want is for the tip of the lower looper to come very close to the scarf of the needle (about .1mm or the distance of a piece of copy machine paper), but we do not want the tip of the looper to actually touch the needle. If the tip of the looper touches the needle it will cause rapid wear of the looper tip. Clearance of less than .1mm but not actually hitting the needle this is acceptable but if the tip of the looper is hitting the needle then it will need to be adjusted.
- **Excessive Clearance** - If the tip of the lower looper is more than .3mm away from the scarf of the needle (2 or three pieces of paper). This is too much clearance and can cause missed stitches.

To adjust the lower looper to needle clearance you will need to loosen the lower looper drive arm lock bolt (or screw) and move the lower looper drive arm to the correct position and then re-tighten the screw (or bolt). Make sure that the lower looper timing is not changed because, the same screw (or bolt) is used to adjust both the lower looper to needle clearance and the lower looper timing. Some people prefer to adjust them at the same time.

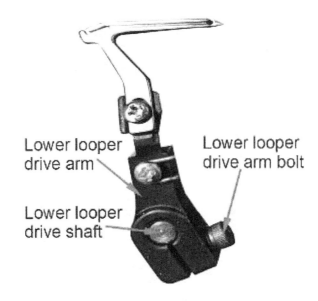

Lower looper drive arm

Lower looper drive arm bolt

Lower looper drive shaft

Lower looper timing

Lower looper timing - With the needle in its lowest position the lower looper should be at or close to its left-most position. The tip of the lower looper should be to the left of the needle by 3mm to 7mm on most machines. For machines with two needles we are talking about the left hand needle. This is shown in the picture below, the lower looper is on the left.

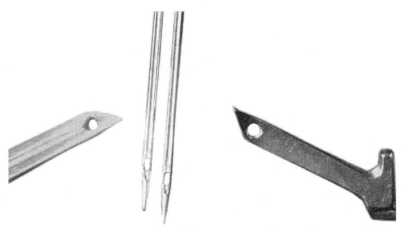

As the hand-wheel is slowly turned in the normal direction of rotation the needle will rise and the tip of the lower looper will move towards the needle. Stop turning when the tip of the lower looper has reached the needle. At this point the needle should have raised about 3mm from its lowest position. The tip of the lower looper should be in the central area of the scarf of the needle as shown in the picture below. The tip of the lower looper must go through the scarf of the needle to catch the needle thread or the stitch will not form correctly.

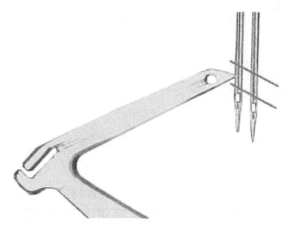

To adjust the lower looper timing you will need to loosen the lower looper drive arm bolt (or screw) and move the lower looper drive arm to the correct position and then re-tighten the screw (or bolt). The lower looper drive arm bolt can be seen in the picture below.

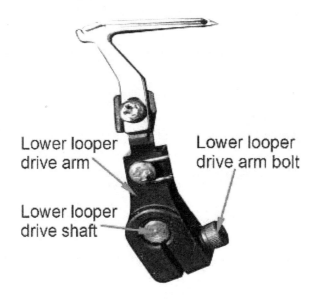

Lower looper drive arm

Lower looper drive arm bolt

Lower looper drive shaft

Make sure that the lower looper to needle clearance is correct before re-tightening, the same screw (or bolt) is used to adjust both the lower looper timing and the lower looper to needle clearance.

After you adjust the lower looper timing you must check the clearance between the tip of the upper looper and the eye area of the lower looper. This is shown in the picture below. The tip of the upper looper must pass through the undercut area of the lower looper and must not hit the protruding area of the lower looper around the eye. If you find that the tip of the upper looper is hitting the lower looper you may have to slightly readjust the lower looper timing to correct the problem. In most cases the lower looper can be adjusted in such a way as to balance the adjustments and achieve correct timing of the lower and upper loopers.

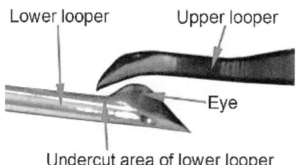

Lower looper

Upper looper

Eye

Undercut area of lower looper

Upper looper clearance

There are two upper looper clearances and they are interrelated, upper looper to lower looper clearance and upper looper to needle clearance. Both are adjusted by loosening the upper looper lock screw and moving the upper looper and then re-tightening the screw. You must check both clearances and balance the adjustment to achieve the best result for both. If you can not achieve a satisfactory balance you may need to replace the upper looper or you may have upper looper drive parts that are worn out, bent or some other problem.

Upper looper to lower looper clearance - Start with the needle in the lowest position and slowly turn the handwheel in the normal direction of rotation until the tip of the upper looper is just passing by the lower looper. This is shown in the picture below on the left. The clearance between the tip of the upper looper and the lower looper should be more than .1mm (or one piece of copy machine paper). The tip of the upper looper should not touch the lower looper at any point. In the picture below on the right you can see that the tip of the upper looper is catching the thread from the lower looper. The tip of the upper looper must be close enough to the lower looper to reliably catch the thread, if it is too far away it will not catch the thread.

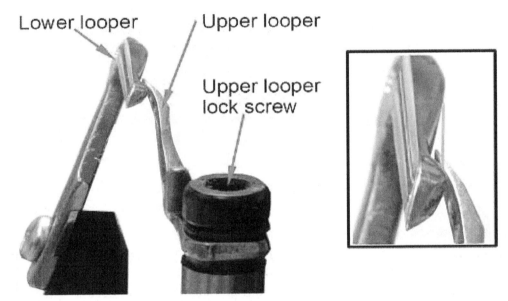

Upper looper to needle clearance - Start with the needle in the highest position. Turn the hand-wheel in the normal direction of rotation until the tip of the needle (or needles) is half way across the scarf of the upper looper. Check the clearance between the tip of the needle (or needles) and the scarf of the upper looper. The clearance should be more than .1mm (one piece of copy machine paper). The picture below shows the clearance being checked.

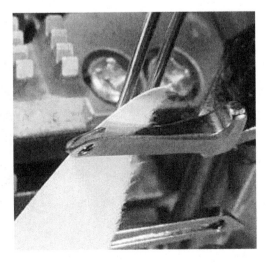

The upper looper must be close enough to the needle so that the needle can catch the thread from the upper looper as it moves down toward the fabric. This is shown in the picture below, you can see the needles catching the green thread from the upper looper. To summarize the upper looper should not touch the needle but be close enough so that the needle can catch the upper looper thread.

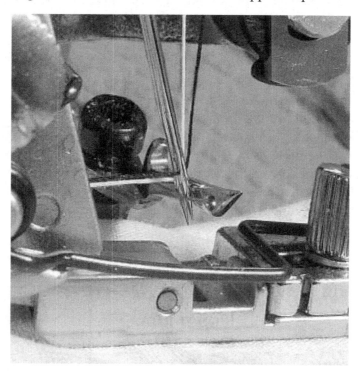

Upper looper timing

Turn the handwheel until the needle is in the highest position. The upper looper should be low enough so that the tip of the needle can go over the upper looper thread. On some machines like the one in the picture below you can see the tips of the needles through the upper looper eye hole, but the needle will just barley go over the thread. As you continue to turn the handwheel the needle should go between the upper looper and the upper looper thread as shown in the picture above.

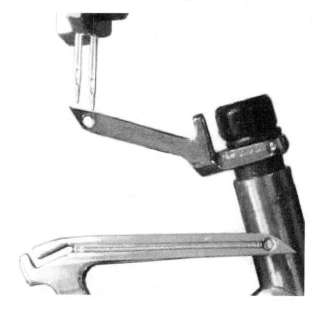

To adjust the upper looper timing loosen the upper looper drive arm lock bolt and rotate the upper looper drive arm to the correct position and then re-tighten the bolt. The upper looper drive bolt is shown in the picture below.

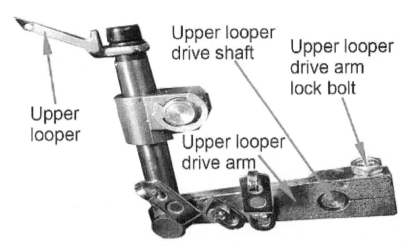

After you adjust the upper looper timing you must check the clearance between the tip of the upper looper and the eye area of the lower looper. This is shown in the picture below. The tip of the upper looper must pass through the undercut area of the lower looper and must not hit the protruding area of the lower looper around the eye. If you find that the upper looper is hitting the lower looper you may have to slightly readjust the lower looper timing to correct the problem.

It is much more common for the lower looper adjustment to come out of adjustment and in most cases the lower looper can be adjusted in such a way as to balance the adjustments and achieve correct timing of the lower and upper loopers.

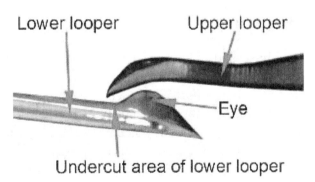

111

Maintenance & Repair

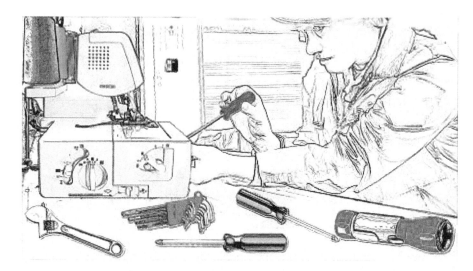

This chapter covers the basics of serger maintenance and was written with a generic machine in mind. Sergers differ from model to model. The procedures in this chapter may not exactly apply to your machine. Use your better judgment and if any part of the procedures do not seem appropriate for your machine you should stop and obtain a service manual for your specific model of machine.

Maintenance Preliminaries

Should I do my own maintenance?

Sergers are more difficult to adjust and maintain than sewing machines because they are more complicated. If you are proficient at adjusting and maintaining sewing machines you can probably learn to adjust and maintain sergers but you should start with sewing machines first before jumping into sergers if you have no experience. I recommend going as far and you feel comfortable and taking your time. Although it is unlikely, it is possible to damage your machine or injure yourself. If you get in over your head and the machine is not functional then take it to a service shop or call a sewing machine mechanic. Most small companies that use industrial machines will try to do as much of the repair and adjustment work as possible, but call a sewing machine mechanic when they can't solve a problem or need major work done.

Is my machine worth fixing?

Before you spend a lot of time and money on repairing an old machine keep in mind that the cost of new sergers has been dropping and that really great sergers are available at inexpensive prices. For the home market you can now get a Brother 1034d for $181 on amazon. For the industrial market you can get a Siruba 700K series machine for $850 through on-line sellers. Sometimes it is a better idea to sell the old machine and buy a new one, especially if you have limited time and must have a machine to do your work. On the other hand you may find repairing and adjusting sergers fun and rewarding and if you are mechanically skilled you may be able to do it without spending a lot of your time.

Service manuals

A service manual is a manual that is written for a specific model of machine and is written by the manufacturer of that machine. The service manual gives detailed instructions for doing adjustments including information such as clearances and adjustment procedures.

In contrast to a service manual this book gives instructions that are generic in nature and are intended to teach general troubleshooting and maintenance skills. This book is not intended to be a replacement for a service manual, although you should be able to use the information in this book to help troubleshoot and do maintenance on most machines.

An advantage to having a service manual is that you can look at each task before you start (like replacing the hook assembly for instance) and see if you really want to do it your self or if it looks too difficult or requires special tools. Some tasks may be better left to a sewing machine mechanic or service shop.

Obtaining service manuals - Some brands will sell a service manual to a consumer while other brands will only sell service manuals to a sewing machine repair shop. If your brand will not sell you a service manual you may be able to buy one from an on-line company that specializes in service manuals (there are many of them). Also try companies that specialize in selling sewing machine parts, they will often sell service manuals as well. Sometimes you can download service manuals for old machines free of charge on-line.

Maintenance intervals

There are two types of cleaning and lubrication; routine and deep. The difference is that routine cleaning and lubrication only takes a few minutes and should be done at regular intervals. Routine cleaning and lubrication does not require a major disassembly of the machine. Deep cleaning and lubrication requires more dis-assembly and is done every two to eight years or during repairs when the machine is partially disassembled anyway.

Home machines - Home sergers should be cleaned and oiled after every 12 hours of actual running time or every 2 years which ever comes first. This depends on the fabric and thread, some fabrics and threads cause more lint, if you notice a lot of lint build up in the machine then it will need to be cleaned and oiled sooner.

Industrial machines - Industrial machines should be cleaned after every 12 hours of actual running time. This depends on the fabric and thread, some fabrics and threads cause more lint, if you notice a lot of lint build up in the machine then it will need to be cleaned sooner. Most industrial machines with forced oil systems and oil reservoirs are automatically oiled and do not require additional oil. The oil in the oil system should be changed every six months for heavy use, every year for medium use and every 2 to 4 years for light use. If the oil is getting darker in color it should be changed (if it looks dirty). If your machine has an oil filter change it after every 2nd oil change. If there are any bearings or other areas of metal to metal contact that do not get oiled by the oiling system then oil those points after every 12 hours of run time or every 2 years which ever comes first.

About oiling and lubrication

In this section we will go over specifics of oiling, for information about types of oil and grease to use in sergers see the section "Oil for sergers & overlock machines" later in this chapter.

The picture below is an example of some metal to metal and plastic to metal bearing surfaces that require oil. If you look closely at the picture you will see that some of the bearings have no visible oil around their outer edges (the part you can see). For these dry looking bearings you should start with two drops of oil and let the oil seep into the bearing for a few seconds. If the bearing still looks dry then add another drop until you can see a slight hint of oil around the outer edge of the bearing. The bearings in the picture labeled as "Oil is visible" have some oil that you can see. For these bearings you need to determine if the oil looks old and thick or looks more like new oil. If the oil looks old and thick you should add a drop or two. If the oil looks thin and new you can pass over that bearing, no oil is needed. The bearings in the picture had oil that was kind of thick so I added a drop or two of oil. If you are not sure it is best to add a drop of oil, this can't hurt anything.

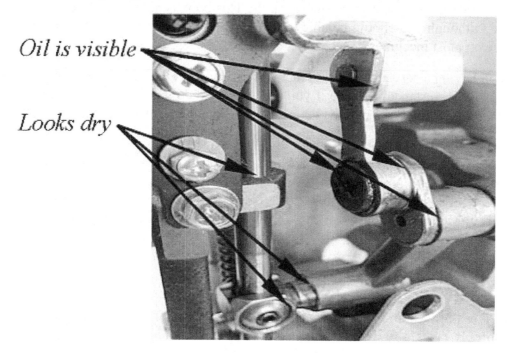

Special concern - Of special concern are belts, electronics, motors and gears:

- Belts and electronics - Do not get oil on belts or drip it into electronic parts or onto circuit boards. Clean up excess oil with a cloth and q-tips.
- Motors - Don't oil the motor unless your owners manual tells you to do so. In general you don't need to oil the motor during a basic clean and oil. If you are doing a deep cleaning and oiling some motors may require oiling, see the sections "Home motors" or "Industrial motors" later in this chapter.
- Gears - will usually need grease and not oil. You can usually tell by looking to see there is already grease present. Just put a few dabs of grease on the gears and then rotate the handwheel to make sure that all of the teeth have some grease. For detailed information about Grease see the section "Grease for sergers & overlock machines" later in this chapter.

Before starting lubrication read the following guidelines and determine what type of oil system your machine has, each type requires different handling.

Machines with a manual oil system - Most home machines and some industrial machines have a manual oil system in which each bearing must be oiled by hand.

- Put a drop or two of oil in the areas that your owners manual tells you to oil. If you have an older machine and do not have an owners manual then oil all bearing surfaces that you can see. Bearing surfaces are any place that moves when the machine is running and has metal to metal contact such as the needle bar, linkages, shafts, etc. Some moving parts in modern machines are made from a kind of hard nylon (a type of plastic). These parts typically are lubricated the same as metal parts.
- If you see gears that have grease, you do should not oil them or if the grease looks dry then use one or two drops of oil.

- Over oiling will cause oil to drip from your machine and make a mess, but otherwise will not harm your machine unless you get oil into the motor. On most bearings if you put in a few drops of oil you will see a little oil around the edges of the bearing surface and that tells you that it has enough oil. If the bearing is really dry it will take in more oil, if the bearing already has oil then just a drop or two will be enough.

Machines with a wick type oil system - Some older home machines and some industrial machines have a wick type oil system. The wick is inside the machine and looks like heavy string or clothing line rope. There are usually a few wicks originating from one or more common oil points (holes) at the top of the machine and then going to each area with bearings or gears. The oil follows the wicks from the oil hole to the bearings so that each bearing does not have to be manually oiled individually.

- The advantage of the oil wick system is that 6 or so drops of oil can be added to each oil hole every few days of use, and then the wick system will slowly supply oil to the bearings for several days. The machine does not have to be opened for periodic oiling. See the owners manual for your machine for information about where the oil points are and how much oil is needed.

Machines with a forced oil system - Most industrial machines have forced oil lubrication systems complete with a built in automatic oil pump and oil pan.

- These machines do not need manual lubrication or only need manual lubrication on a few parts. If there are gears that are inside the forced oil lubricated areas then of course those gears do not need grease because they get oil from the forced oil system. See the owners manual for your machine for complete information about what parts if any need manual oiling on machines with a forced oil system.

Lubed for life?

Many newer home machines (less than 20 years) are so called "lubricated for life". If you have one of these machines the manufacturer will state in the owners manual that the machine does not require lubrication or that only one or two places such as the looper driver shaft need lubrication.

- Actually there is no such thing as lubricated for life, what they really mean is that the machine is intended to have a limited service life and that the lubrication should last for the intended service life. However, some of these machines can last much longer then the intended service life. For average home use "Lubed for life" = "Lubed for 5 or 10 years"
- The lubrication that is used in these machines is a synthetic or other very high quality lubricant and actually does last a very long time.
- My advice concerning "lubed for life" machines is to inspect the bearing areas that you can see (like the needle bar area) and see if you can see any lubricant around the bearings. If so, does it look reasonably fresh or does it look dried or dirty? If you can see lubricant that looks OK then you can do nothing or put in a drop of oil. If the lubricant that you see looks dry, dirty or you can't see any lubricant at all then oil normally, put in enough oil so that you can see that it is well lubricated.
- Do not over oil these machines because you do not want to flush out all of the original lubricant, most of the time the original lubricant starts to get thick and a drop or two of oil will thin it out and restore proper lubrication.

Clearances and units of measurement

- Sewing machine parts are measured in inches (the imperial measurement system) or in millimeters (the metric system). Older (vintage) machines made in the USA, England and Canada and most vintage Singer machines use the imperial system. Asian, European and all newer machines use the metric system.
- It is easy to convert from imperial to metric, 1 inch is 25.4 millimeters.
- When measuring clearances or diameters of small parts in the imperial system the unit of measurement is .001 inches. This is referred to as a "thousandth" or a "mil". For example if we measure an average human hair it will be about .003 inches which is said as "3 thousandths" (or you can say "3 mils").
- When measuring clearances or diameters of small parts in the metric system the unit of measurement is .001 millimeters. This is referred to as a micrometer. For example if we measure an average human hair it will be about 76 micrometers.

Oil for sergers & overlock machines

For sergers and overlock machines you should use sewing machine oil. You can buy sewing machine oil at any sewing machine store or even at Walmart. "Sewing machine oil" is actually a clear or white colored spindle oil. This type of oil stains fabric as little as possible and has very low friction properties to reduce wear on the machine. Spindle oil was developed for high speed industrial milling machines, but is also used in sewing machines because it has the correct properties needed for low friction and long life.

Do not use "3 in 1 oil", any kind of "household oil", WD40 or automotive oil in a serger - These oils have solvent mixed into them or are too thick. The solvent is used so that household oils will penetrate into rusty hinges and locks. In a serger the solvent will evaporate over time and the oil will become very thick and gum up the machine. If you did use house hold oil in your machine you should re-oil with sewing machine oil and the new oil will flush out the household oil and everything will be back to normal. Never use motor oil in a serger, it is far too thick and will make the machine run slow and possibly interfere with the action of some parts.

Oil Bottles - Get one of the small 4 ounce plastic bottles with the long pull-out tube like the one pictured below if you can, it makes oiling much easier. The bottles with a pull out tube are more expensive but it is worth the cost to get the pull out tube. With the long tube you can put the oil exactly where it is needed in the right amount, otherwise it is hard to get the oil into the right place and you end up dripping a lot of extra oil into the machine and all over your table and floor. Sew machine oil comes in small bottles, pints, quarts, liters, half gallons, gallons and five gallon drums.

Viscosity Grade - (VG) is the term used to specify the thickness of a liquid (in this case oil). ISO is the International Standards Organization. "ISO VG 15 spindle oil" is therefore a spindle oil with an ISO viscosity grade of 15.

For home sergers - Sewing machine oil that is used for home sergers is a white spindle oil and is usually about ISO VG 15 viscosity. This is what you get when you go to Walmart or your local sewing machine store and get the bottles labeled as "sewing machine oil". Normally they don't give the viscosity rating on the label and it could be between VG 10 to VG 22. This range is fine for home sergers and some industrial machines.

For industrial overlock machines - the owners manual of your machine will usually specify a certain type of oil to use. If possible it is a good idea to use the type of oil that is recommended. Most industrial overlock machines use ISO VG 22 sewing machine oil. If you don't have an owners manual or oil specifications for your machine then ISO VG 22 or ISO VG 15 sewing machine oil should work fine for most machines.

Brands of oil

- **Generic** - This type of oil will have "Sewing Machine Oil", "White Sewing Machine Oil", "High Speed Sewing Machine Oil" or "Lilly White Sewing Machine Oil" on the label. It may or may not have a viscosity grade listed on the label, if not then it is probably ISO VG 10 or ISO VG 22. The label may also say "Paraffin Oil", "Mineral Oil" , "White Oil", "Petroleum Oil" or a blend of any of them. These are all generic terms for the same thing and have no specific meaning.
- **Synthetic** - Synthetic oils are available in the correct viscosities for sewing machines but are more expensive and do not seem to have much of an advantage in this application because sewing machines do not operate at high temperatures where synthetic oils hold up better.
- **Juki**
  - New Defrix oil No.1 - this is an ISO VG 7 oil, you can substitute an ISO 10.
  - Juki Machine Oil 7 - this is an ISO VG 7 oil, you can substitute an ISO 10 oil.
  - Juki Machine Oil 18 - this is an ISO VG18 oil, you can substitute an ISO 22 oil.
- **Mobil**
  - Velocite SM Series - These oils are blended specifically for sewing machines and are clear white. The oils in this series are: Velocite SM 10 - ISO VG 10, Velocite SM 15 - ISO VG 15, Velocite SM 22 - ISO VG 22
  - Velocite Oil Numbered Series - **Watch out these oils are confusing**, as you can see the Number names are not the same as the viscosities! These are high speed spindle oils for machine tools but are often used for sewing machines. The color may not be as white as the sewing machine oils (or maybe it is?) but the lubrication quality should be the same. The oils in this series and viscosities are: Velocite No 6 = ISO VG 10, Velocite No 8 = ISO VG 15, Velocite No 10 = ISO VG 22
- **Other brands of spindle oil** - These oils are high speed spindle oils for machine tools but can also be used in sewing machines. All of the following oils have names that are the same as their ISO viscosities. The color may not be as white as the sewing machine oils but the lubrication quality should be the same.
  - BP® Spindle Oil 10, BP® Spindle Oil 22
  - Shell Spindle 10, Spindle 22
  - Exxon Spinesstic 10, Spinesstic 22
  - Chevron CP Oil 10 and CP Oil 22
  - Castrol Spindle 10, Spindle 22

Grease for sergers & Overlock Machines

For sergers and overlock machines a general purpose lithium grease or a white lithium grease work well. The only practical difference between the two is that general purpose is kind of a yellow or brown color and the white type is an off-white or cream color. High temperature wheel bearing grease should not be used in sewing machines because it is too thick at low temperatures.

- **General purpose lithium grease** - is available at any automotive parts store. Get the most inexpensive type, the low or medium temperature type used for door hinges, body part lubrication and low temperature bearings. Do not get any of the more expensive types of higher temperature grease because they are too thick and will make your machine run slowly!
- **White lithium grease** - is available at hardware stores and may be available at automotive parts stores. This grease is similar to general purpose lithium grease but is white in color.
- **High temperature wheel bearing grease** - should not be used in sergers and overlock machines because it is too thick at low temperatures and will slow the machine down.
- **Marine or water proof grease** - Too thick for sergers and overlock machines.

Basic cleaning and oiling

For basic cleaning and oiling follow the instructions in the owners manual for your machine, every machine is different. Some newer machines do not require oiling or only require oiling of a few parts. If your machine has had heavy use or you want to do a complete cleaning and lubrication job then see the sections " disassembly" and "Cleaning and lubrication" further in this chapter.

Basic cleaning

- Follow the thread path and clean lint and old thread from all thread guides.
- Get some heavy thread or light string and run it through the tension disks to clean out any lint from the tension disks. You do this kind of like using floss to floss your teeth. Be careful not to damage the tension spring while you clean the tension disks.
- Remove the needle plate (if possible). Use an old tooth brush and Q-tips to clean lint and dirt from the feed dogs and feed dog area. You can also use a cleaning brush (they look like a small paint brush).
- Open the looper cover (or covers). Use the tooth brush and Q-tips to clean the loopers and looper area. A small paint brush also works well.

Basic oiling

- Put a few drops of oil in the areas that your owners manual tells you to oil. If you have an older machine and do not have an owners manual then oil all bearing surfaces that you can see. Bearing surfaces are any place that moves and has metal to metal contact such as the needle bar, linkages, shafts, etc. If you see gears that have grease, you do should not oil them or if the grease looks dry then use one or two drops of oil.

- Over oiling will cause oil to drip from your machine and make a mess but otherwise will not harm your machine. On most bearings if you put in a few drops of oil you will see a little oil around the edges of the bearing surface and that tells you that it has enough oil. If the bearing is really dry it will take in more oil, if the bearing already has oil then just a drop or two will be enough.

- Don't oil the motor unless your owners manual tells you to (in general you don't need to oil the motor during a basic clean and oil, we will get into oiling motors later in this chapter).

Disassembly

If your machine is under warranty then opening the case may violate your warranty. If this is a concern to you then read your warranty before proceeding.

Home machines

For full cleaning, lubrication and for repair the inner parts of the machine must be exposed. Most older metal machines have a few simple covers that can be removed to expose the lubrication points of the machine. Some newer plastic machines have easy to remove covers, but most newer plastic machines need to have the outer case removed or have large sections of the outer case removed to assess the inner parts.

How far into the machine do you really need to go? That depends, my thoughts are as follows:

- Machines more than 20 years old need all bearings oiled periodically. These machines are usually built with access panels or body covers that are easy to remove so that you have access to the parts that will need oil.

- Some machines less then 20 years old may be very difficult to open for service and may require the entire outer case of the machine to be removed because they do not have access panels except the bottom panel. The bottom panel on most machines comes off with a 4 or 6 screws. Most of the machines with cases that are difficult to remove use some type of long lasting synthetic lubrication on the inner parts (see the section "lubricated for life" below). What I usually do is take off the bottom panel and inspect the bearing surfaces that I can access to see if those areas look like they are lubricated or not. If the bearings that I can see look lubricated and the machine does not show any signs of needing lubrication (running slow or making inappropriate noises) and if the machine otherwise looks clean and in good shape then I will assume that the bearings that I can't see are also OK and will not take apart the entire machine.

- Some machines less than 25 years old do have easy to remove panels for access to all internal parts. In this case I usually can't stop my self from taking off all the panels and inspecting, cleaning and lubricating if needed but you may chose to open them on an as needed basis if you are not as curious as I am.

How to remove panels on machines with access panels - The covers remove with a few screws exposing the internal parts of the machine. There is a big difference between how machines are disassembled between manufacturers, if it is not obvious how to gain access to oil and clean the machine then you should get an owners manual for instructions. If it is not covered in the owners manual you should obtain a service manual for your machine.

How to open newer plastic case machines without access panels - On this type of machine the case is usually split and has two halves, a front half and a back half. Most machines have the screws on the back and bottom of the case but sometimes there could be screws hidden in strange places. On some machines there are also tabs and screws under labels or under plastic covers. First remove the visible screws that look like they hold the case together and then try to take off the front or back of the case. If the case will not open then gently separate the sections of the case that will move and try to figure out what remaining screws or tabs are still preventing it from opening. There is usually a screw or tab that you did not see or that was hidden. Some cases are quite difficult to open. If you can't figure out how to open the case then do not force it open, you may need to get a service manual that will show you how to open the case.

Document what you are doing - As you are removing covers (or any parts) from the machine or taking the case apart you should lay the parts out along with the corresponding screws in such a way that you can remember where they came from so that you can put the machine back together again. Sometimes I lay the parts out on top of paper with notes or write post-it notes and stick them on the relevant parts so I can remember how to reassemble complicated machines. Another good idea is to take a few pictures during disassembly to help you remember where parts should go.

Re-assembly - Most of the time re-assembly is just the opposite of disassembly. Don't over tighten screws that attach plastic parts or plastic panels, the screws for these parts just need to be snug but not as tight as for metal parts.

Industrial machines

Industrial machines have easy to remove access panels to allow you to service and adjust the machines, most machines have access doors that open with a latch or knob. The panels that are attached with screws are usually only attached with few screws that are easy to identify. Most of the internal parts on industrial machines are usually in the area that is lubricated with the forced oil lubrication system. These parts do not need to be lubricated or cleaned because of the oil system. Most adjustments can be made without opening the machine, unless there is something that needs repair you do not need to open the internal areas of the machine that are lubricated by the oil system. If you do need to open the machine the oil system will usually have to be drained. See the owners manual for your machine for instructions on how to drain the oil system.

Deep cleaning & lubrication

Clean, inspect, tighten.

- **Start any where** - Go through the machine (there is no particular order needed) and clean, inspect, tighten and lubricate the machine. I like to start with the needle bar area first, then the top of the machine and finally the bottom of the machine.
- **Cleaning** - Use a Q-tip, old tooth brush, lint brush, rag, etc to clean lint, dust, dirt and old lube from all parts of the machine. Clean lint from all critical areas such as around the feed dogs, loopers and cutters. You may need to remove the needle plate for better access.
- **Check and inspect** - Check for any screws that may be loose and make sure they are tight. In particular check the drive screws associated with the needle bar and loopers because if these screws are loose the machine will loose its timing and need to be readjusted. Also check the screws that attach the cutting blades. Check all parts for proper operation while you are turning the hand-wheel and oiling the machine.
- **Run the machine and listen** - The machine should run smooth, if you hear something that sounds loose then you may want to investigate and see if something needs to be tightened.

- **Check for free running** - Older home machines and all industrial machines should run freely with a minimum of effort required to turn the hand wheel. Some newer home machines have some internal drag by design. The motor will add drag and sometimes it is hard to tell if the machine is dragging or not when the motor is connected. If you suspect that the machine is dragging you may want to remove the drive belt so that you can rotate the hand wheel without the motor adding drag to see if the machine is dragging or running freely. On machines with gear drive it may be difficult to disconnect the motor but on most belt drive machines it is easy to loosen the motor adjustment screw (or bolt) and remove the drive belt. For older home machines and all industrial machines If you find that the machine is dragging then go through the entire machine and make sure that all moving parts are lubricated properly, most of the time when a machine is dragging it is because some bearing is not lubricated. Also listen, you may be able to hear the part that is dragging.

Lubricating home machines

- Put a few drops of oil in the areas that your owners manual tells you to oil. If you have an older machine and do not have an owners manual then oil all bearings and surfaces that move against another surface. Bearing surfaces are any place that moves and has metal to metal contact or plastic to metal contact such as the needle bar, linkages, shafts, etc.
- Some home sergers have a wick type lubrication system. The wick looks like heavy yarn or clothing line rope. There are usually a few wicks originating from a common oil hole at the top of the machine and then going to each area with bearings or gears. The oil follows the wicks from the oil hole to the bearings. The advantage of the oil wick system is that 6 or so drops of oil can be added to the main oil hole every few days of use, and then the wicks will supply the oil to the bearings. The machine does not have to be opened for periodic oiling.
- Gears will usually need grease. Just put a few dabs of grease on the gears and then rotate the hand-wheel to make sure that all of the teeth have some grease.
- Large rotating rod bearings need oil. Do not grease these bearings or your machine will run slow!
- Over oiling will cause oil to drip from your machine and make a mess but otherwise will not harm your machine. On most bearings if you put in a few drops of oil you will see a little oil around the edges of the bearing surface and that tells you that it has enough oil. If the bearing is really dry it will take in more oil, if the bearing already has oil then just a drop or two will be enough.
- Don't oil the motor unless your owners manual tells you to (in general you don't need to oil the motor during a basic clean and oil. For more complete info on oiling motors see the section "Home motors" or "Industrial motors" later in this chapter.

Lubricating industrial machines

- Most industrial sergers and overlock machines (except some specialized machines) have oil pans and oil systems so they do not need manual lubrication or only need manual lubrication on a few parts. See the owners manual for your machine for complete information about what parts if any need manual oiling. As for industrial motors, most industrial motors have sealed bearings that are lubricated for life. Some very industrial motors (over 50 years) may have bearings that need to be oiled, if you can see an oil hole or oil fitting (small protrusion with a little spring cap on it) on the top of the bearing area then add a few drops of oil.

Drive Belts

Drive belts come in three general types; round belts, v-belts and cogged belts.

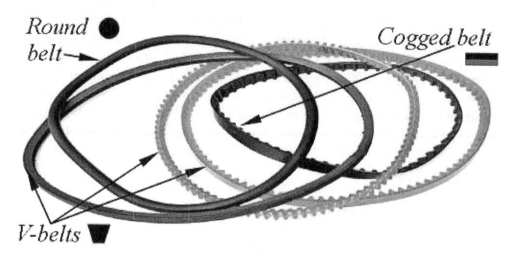

Round belts have a round cross profile (if you cut the belt crosswise and look at the cut end you are looking at the profile). Round belts can be made of rubber or leather and are generally used on older machines. Round belts are the least efficient at transferring power, so after about 1950 manufacturers started using V-belts.

V-belts have a modified "V" profile with angled sides and a flat bottom. They are used on home machines from about 1950-1985 and are still used on some industrial machines. V-belts are better at transmitting power than round belts because the sides have more contact area with the pulley (which also has angled sides). The two lighter colored V-belts shown in the picture below have undercutting to make them more flexible, it may look like they have teeth or cogs but these belts have smooth angled sides and really are V-belts.

Cogged belts have teeth (also called cogs) and require a pulley that has corresponding teeth. They are used on most machines built in the 1990's and later. Cogged belts do not slip because the teeth of the belt interlock with the teeth of the pulley. They are made with a rectangular profile and are thinner and more flexible than V-belts and therefore more efficient at transferring power. The picture below shows a cogged belt and cogged pulley in a modern machine.

Belt Inspection - Look at the belt and see if it is in acceptable condition. If the belt is coming apart or is chewed up you will see it. The surface that you should be most concerned with is the inside surface of the belt that comes in contact with the pulleys. If the inside surface is shiny (this is called glazed) then the belt will slip. In this case the belt should be replaced or you can try to lightly rub it with some 220 grit sand paper to remove the shiny surface. If you do this make sure to take a cloth and remove all the sand paper grit from the belt before trying it on the machine.

Tension adjustment - On most machines the belt is adjusted by tilting or moving the motor on its mounting system. There is usually an adjustment screw or screws to do this. On some machines there are several mounting nuts that must be loosened to adjust the belt. Some older machines have a spring loaded motor mount that does not require adjustment and keeps to belt tension at the correct level automatically.

Belt tightness for V-belts and round belts - If your machine has a smooth drive pulley on the motor (most older machines) then your machine uses a v-belt or a round belt. These belts should be only tight enough to prevent slippage. If belts are too tight they rob power and slow the machine, also over tight belts cause unnecessary bearing wear and premature belt failure. Belts that are too loose slip, cause poor acceleration of the machine and cause the belt to prematurely wear out. Start with the belt too loose and then tighten it until the belt no longer slips under acceleration. The belt should be just tight enough to avoid belt slippage but no tighter. You can test for belt slippage by holding the handwheel and pressing on the foot pedal to run the motor for a second or two. This is called a stall test. In this case a little belt slippage is normal in most cases. While you are sewing, if you notice belt slippage then adjust the belt a little bit tighter until you can sew without belt slippage.

Belt tightness for cogged belts - If your machine has a pulley with teeth or intentions and your belt also has teeth then you have a cogged belt. This type of belt is used on most new machines including all electronic machines. Adjust a cogged belt so that it is not loose but not overly tight either. Real scientific huh? Actually the correct tension depends on several factors including the distance between the pulley and the handwheel and the design of the belt. You want the belt to have enough tension so that the teeth of the motor pulley stay connected with the teeth of the belt and prevent the belt from slipping. If there is too much tension it will cause rapid wear of the motor bearings and the belt. So it is a compromise. If you are not sure you could try to hold the motor pulley from moving and try to turn the hand wheel and see if you can cause the belt to slip. If you can't cause the belt to slip on the motor pulley then the belt is probably tight enough. Make sure that the belt is not too tight, if you pluck the belt like a guitar string it should vibrate at a low frequency like a bass guitar. If it is too tight it will vibrate at a higher frequency.

Home Motors

Caution - Motors use electric power and improper disassembly or repair of motors can cause fire or electric shock. If you do not have experience with motors or electrical work you should find someone with experience to do the work or teach you the proper procedures.

Home machines with universal motors

Older home machines and newer home machines that are not electronic use a universal motor. The universal motor is called "universal" because it can run on both AC power or DC power. The universal motor is relatively small but has a high power output and is quite reliable and easy to manufacture. Universal motors use electric coils (wire) for both the armature (also called the rotor, the part that turns) and the stator (the stationary part of the motor). No permanent magnets are used. There is a commutator and brushes to conduct power from the body of the motor to the rotor. The universal motor shown in the picture below has one of the brush caps visible at the back of the motor on the top, the other cap is in the same position on the bottom.

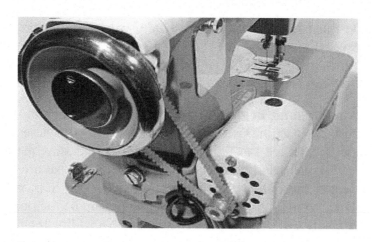

Brushes - The brushes are small parts that conduct electricity to the commutator of the motor as the motor rotates. The brushes slide on the surface of the commutator. Brushes have a long service life, but after many hours they need to be replaced or the motor will loose power and finally stop running. Some motors have 2 small caps on the outside of the motor that can be unscrewed to access the brushes for easy replacement. Other motors require disassembly for brush replacement. Always unplug the machine before removing or replacing brushes. The brushes are made of carbon and graphite and have a spring attached to them as pictured below.

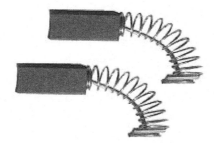

Cleaning - Universal motors can get crudded up with lint, dust and power from the brushes. In most cases the motor can be cleaned without disassembly by using que-tips and a vacuum cleaner to dislodge and suck out the dust.

Wiring - Sometimes the power cord going to the motor becomes rotten and needs to be replaced. In this case the motor may need to be dissembled. You should refer to a qualified service person for this, or someone with experience working on electric motors.

Lubrication - If the machine is going slow check to see if the machine itself is dragging and needs lubrication instead of the motor. Home machines have universal motors or DC motors (see picture above). These motors have brushes and a commutator (sliding electrical contacts) to transfer electricity to the rotor (the part of the motor that spins). You do not want to get oil on the brushes and commutator because the oil will burn and foul the brushes. Also you do not want to get oil on the pulley and drive belt because it will cause the belt to slip and get gummed up. Very carefully add a drop or two to the motor shaft on the side with the pulley (see picture). Rotate the motor (or run the motor at low speed under power) to work the oil into the bearing. Use a Q-tip to remove excess oil that could get onto the pulley and belt. Look to see if the motor shaft is visible on the opposite side from the pulley. If the shaft is visible then add one or two drops of oil to the bearing. If the shaft is not visible then look very carefully to see if there is an oiling hole or if you can see a felt oiling ring. If you see an oil hole or a felt oiling ring you can add a drop or two of oil. If you can not see how to oil the non-pulley side of the motor then if the motor has been running good you can skip oiling that side of the motor. The non-pulley side of the motor gets far less wear and tear then the pulley side and can often go a long time without needing lubrication. If the motor is running bad and you can not figure out how to oil the non-pulley side of the motor then the motor will need to be diss-assembled and serviced. Do not attempt to diss-assemble the motor your self unless you have experience with repairing electric motors, either replace it, take it to a qualified shop or have someone with experience help you.

Replacement motors - If you need to replace the motor of your home sewing machine it is usually better to get a used motor that is exactly the same as your existing motor instead of getting a new generic replacement type motor. This is because the speed, power and torque curves for home sewing machine motors vary a lot from model to model. Your machine was designed to sew well with a specific model of motor, a different motor may not work well with your machine. A badly matched motor can make the machine sluggish or the machine may run too fast and have excessive vibration and lack of control. Also the mounting hardware for general replacement type motors may not fit your machine correctly or the belt may not adjust correctly with the new motor. If you get an original type motor you will not have these problems.

Electronic home machines with DC motors

Electronic home machines use DC motors. DC motors are similar to universal motors but use magnets in the non-rotating part of the motor instead of a stator.

You can put a drop or two of oil on the shaft of these motors if they need lubrication, but otherwise most DC motors used in sewing machines are not serviceable and need to be replaced if they are not working correctly. I have only seen one or two DC motors that had accessible brushes that could be replaced. Replacement DC motors must be the exact type as the original motor, generic replacements will not work. A typical DC motor is pictured below.

Industrial Motors

Industrial clutch motors

No brushes - Clutch motors do not have brushes to wear out or require replacement.

Bearings - Most industrial motors have sealed bearings that are lubricated for life. Some very old industrial motors (over 50 years) may have bearings that need to be oiled, if you can see an oil hole or oil fitting (small protrusion with a little spring cap on it) on the top of the bearing area then add a few drops of sewing machine oil. If the motor is making bearing noise the bearings must be replaced (requires disassembly of the motor).

Clutch assembly lubrication - The clutch engagement arm, linkage to the foot pedal and foot pedal assembly require a few drops of oil to lubricate anywhere there is metal on metal moving parts to insure smooth operation.

Clutch adjustment - Most clutch motors have an adjustment that sets the gap between the clutch disk and the brake pad. If this gap is too tight the machine will lack low speed controllability and will abruptly change from full speed to full stop. The adjustment is usually a bolt head protruding from the clutch area that is turned to change the gap between the disk and the break pad, there is also a lock nut so that the adjustment does not change. You must loosen the lock nut first before making the adjustment and re-tighten after the adjustment. If you are not sure you should get a service manual for your specific motor, there are many configurations.

Tension spring - Clutch motors also have a spring tension adjustment of the peddle return spring that effects the braking behavior of the machine. Try various settings until you like the way the clutch action feels.

Total adjustment - The combination of clutch adjustment and spring tension adjustment effects the way the machine starts and stops and determines the rate of transition from stopped to running and the ability to slip the clutch and achieve lower speed operation. If the machine does not respond the way you like then try various adjustments until you find a setting that is closer to your needs. If you can not adjust the clutch to your liking you may need to get a servo motor, some servo motors have highly customization digital adjustments to dial in the exact response you require. Clutch motors tend to have a limited range of adjustment possible.

Clutch disk - If the clutch engages and disengages roughly the clutch disk may be warped or worn. In this case the disk must be replaced. On most motors the clutch disk looks like a small version (about 100mm in diameter) of an automotive clutch disk and is removed by separating the clutch housing from the motor after removing several screws or bolts. There are many models of clutch disk, you must get a replacement disk that is compatible with your motor. I usually bring the old disk to my local industrial sewing machine dealer so that I can match the new disk to the old one and make sure I am getting the right replacement disk. If a replacement disk is not available then sometimes you can clean up the surface of the old disk by sanding it down with 220 grit sand paper. The friction surface of most disks is made from a cork material or similar material.

Lubrication - See the section on "Lubricating industrial motors" earlier in this chapter under "Cleaning & lubrication".

Industrial servo motors

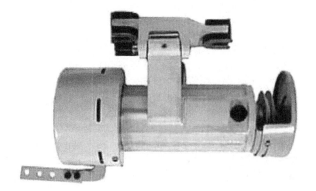

General - Servo motors have a built in computer that monitors and controls the motor. Because the computer is controlling the motor a clutch is not needed. The foot pedal of the machine is connected to a sensor that tells the computer what the pedal position is. The computer then regulates the power going to the motor as needed. Servo motors run only when the machine is actually sewing so they consume much less power than a clutch motor. Most servo motors are more complicated then other types of motors because of the sensors and computer control electronics. Do not attempt to service a servo motor unless you have prior experience and knowledge of electronics.

Bearings - The bearings are the sealed type and do not require lubrication. If the motor is making bearing noise the bearings must be replaced (requires disassembly of the motor).

Brushes - Some servo motors have brushes (like the one pictured above). There are some types that are accessible through brush caps on the outside of the motor but other types require disassembly of the motor. The brushes last a long time. If you suspect that your motor has brushes and they need replacement you should get a service manual for you specific motor or send your motor in for repair.

Adjustment - Servo motors have adjustable top speeds using a knob (or digital adjustment depending on the model) and can be set to run in reverse with a reverse switch or setting. Some servo motors have other adjustments that are made with a digital control panel such as acceleration rate, deceleration rate, acceleration knee, low speed response, etc. See the operators manual for your specific motor to learn about these adjustments, they are different on each model.

Lubrication - See the section on "Lubricating industrial motors" earlier in this chapter under "Cleaning & lubrication".

Repairs

Causes of common problems

The most common cause of problems are traumatic events and loose parts. When a new serger leaves the factory it goes through a series of checks similar to the checklist we went through in the chapter on troubleshooting and all needed adjustments are made so that it is running optimally. After all adjustments are made the factory technicians will tighten all screws so that the machine will stay in adjustment. Sergers will normally stay in adjustment for many years of use unless a traumatic event causes them to come out of adjustment. Normal wear will not usually cause a serger to come out of adjustment.

Loose parts are also a cause of problems. Loose parts can cause a traumatic event. For example if the needle comes loose it can collide with the needle plate or the lower looper. When this happens the needle bar is obstructed and suddenly stops, but the rest of the moving parts of the machine try to keep going. This is causes whiplash and can put a tremendous stress on the parts directly or indirectly connected to the part that stopped. Loose parts are sometimes caused by the operator or a repair person insufficiently tightening screws after an adjustment or repair is made.

Traumatic events are as follows:

- **The needle colliding with the needle plate** - This is usually caused by the operator pulling or pushing the fabric instead of letting the feed dogs do the work. It can also be caused by needle deflection while going over thick seams or going around curves. Machines are supposed to be designed to endure a needle being broken without coming out of adjustment but this is not always the case and some needle breaks are more traumatic to the machine then others. A needle break can cause the needle bar height to come out of adjustment.
- **The lower looper jamming with thread** - This can cause the lower looper timing come out of adjustment or bent.

- **The needle bending and catching the lower looper** - This can cause the lower looper timing to come out of adjustment and can also cause the lower looper to needle clearance to be out of adjustment. It can also cause the lower looper to become bent.
- **Upper looper colliding with the lower looper** - This can be cause by a thread jam or by the fabric if it is mis-fed or gets caught in the upper looper. This can cause the upper looper timing to become out of adjustment, the lower looper timing to become out of adjustment or the upper or lower loopers to become bent.

Most of the above events will cause a single part to come out of adjustment or become bent.

Finding bent, loose or broken parts

If you suspect that your machine has suffered a traumatic event or has broken, bent or loose parts then proceed as follows:

- Turn the hand wheel in the normal direction of rotation while watching the machine go through a few cycles (one cycle of the machine is one rotation of the hand wheel). Stop if there is difficulty turning the hand-wheel or if any of the parts collide with each other or are obstructed from moving in any way. Watch the upper looper, lower looper and needle in particular. If you detect any colliding parts then stop turning the hand-wheel. Colliding parts are caused by something being seriously out of adjustment or by bent parts (or both).
- If you can clearly see that you have a bent part (such as a bent upper looper) then replace the bent part (or parts). After you have replaced the bent parts and you can rotate the machine without any colliding parts then proceed troubleshooting the machine and adjustment.
- If you can't see that any parts are bent then try to adjust the colliding parts so that there is no collision. If the parts are indeed not bent you should be able to adjust them and resolve the collision. If you can't adjust the parts to resolve the collision then one or more parts are bent and you will need to replace them.
- If there is difficulty turning the hand-wheel but you are sure that there is no collision of the loopers or needle and you can't find any other obstructed parts such as feed dogs, cutters or take up levers then your machine probably has an internal problem such as a frozen bearing and needs to be disassembled.

Fixing or replacing parts

- **Visibly bent parts** - If you can see that a part (like the upper looper for instance) is clearly bent then replace it before proceeding. Sometimes it is possible to bend a bent part back into alignment but this is often an iffy proposition. If you are skilled at bending metal parts then give it a try but otherwise it is probably a better idea to just replace the part. Parts like loopers are made of very hard metal and tend to crack and break before they will bend. Sometimes bending can cause cracks that you don't see and will weaken the part so that it will break later.
- **Parts that will not adjust** - Sometimes a part becomes slightly bent but it is not clearly visible that the part is bent. In this case you may find that you can not adjust the machine. If this is the case then you have to take your best guess as to which part is causing the problem and replace that part. If you still cannot properly adjust the machine then replace the next most probable part and so on until the machine will adjust properly. Normally there is only a single bent part.
- **Loose parts** - Try to tighten loose parts in the same position that they were in before becoming loose, this will help minimize the required adjustments to get the machine back into adjustment.

Frozen parts

Under certain conditions moving parts such as shafts or linkages can become frozen. A frozen or seized part will not move as if it is permanently attached to the machine of another part. This happens when bearings run out of oil or grease and water or humidity cause corrosion or oxidation of the bearing surfaces. This causes the surfaces to bond as if some strong glue were injected into the bearing.

Sometimes it is possible to free frozen parts, other times they must be forcefully removed by impact (using a hammer) or by drilling them out. This usually results in damage so the part will need to be replaced. To free frozen parts first put oil into the offending bearing and let it soak for several hours to several days (the longer it soaks the better chance you have or freeing the part). After the oil soaks in try to move the part back and forth (using pliers if needed). If you can get even a little movement then you can add more oil and continue to rock the part back and forth so that you get more motion. If you are as gentle as possible and increase the movement of the part a little at a time you may be able to un-freeze the part with little or no damage.

Fixing parts that are not available

Most parts for sergers are easy to get and relatively inexpensive, but every so often you will come across a part that is not available or very hard to get. In this case you have three choices, 1. Have a machine shop make a part for you or repair your broken part. This can be expensive. 2. Buy a used machine to use as a parts donor machine. This can sometimes be a very good option if you can find one at a reasonable price. 3. Make or repair the part yourself.

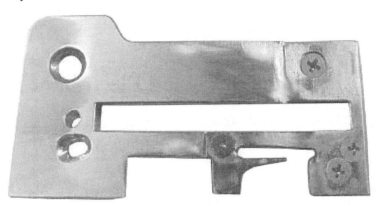

At first thought it may seem impossible to make parts yourself, but actually it is not that difficult in some cases. Many times you do not have to start from scratch, if you have a similar machine that you are using for parts you may be able to get a part that is close and modify that part. The picture above shows a needle plate for a serger that was damaged (the stitch finger was broken off and the plate was cracked). The plate was repaired using hand tools and an electric drill by grafting a new section made form stainless steel (shown on the left side of the picture). The stainless steel came from a kitchen utensil (a spatula). The stainless steel was cut to size using a hack saw and then filed smooth with a hand file and sandpaper. The whole process took about 4 hours and the repaired plate worked satisfactory in the machine.

To make or modify simple parts you need the following tools and equipment:

- Basic tools - Files, pliers, vise, hack saw, work bench, sand paper, spray paint, etc.
- Electric hand tools - Electric drill, Dremel tool, etc.
- Nice to have - Drill press, bench grinder, metal lathe or milling machine.

Following are some guidelines for working with various materials that sewing machine parts are made from:

Metal - Depending on the type, some metals like aluminum are quite soft and easy to cut, drill and file.

Iron is harder than aluminum but still not difficult to work with. Steel is a harder metal and can be time consuming to cut and file but is the most durable and is often used for moving parts. In some instances you may be able to use aluminum to replace steel depending on if the part comprises a bearing surface (In general aluminum does not do well for bearing surfaces that receive heavy wear). You can get metal of all types from your local hardware store. Some types of steel, like the steel used for the hook is high carbon steel and is hardened or chromed. This type of metal is very difficult to work with and these parts are better to replace then to attempt to repair.

Plastic - In general plastic is much easier to work with then metal because it is a much softer material. You can use the same tools for plastic that you do with metal. Plastic can sometimes be a problem to glue because some types of plastic do not take glue very well. One option is to melt the plastic with a soldering iron to form a weld or joint. Make sure to do this outside or with good ventilation and don't breath the plastic smoke or fumes.

Epoxy - In general glue is not very effective for fixing internal sewing machine parts, but works well for cosmetic repairs. One exception to this can be structural epoxy. Structural epoxy is epoxy that is made for the repair of parts or for fabricating parts. An example that is available at a local hardware store is JB Weld. If you go to an industrial parts store like Granger you will find many other types from 3M and other vendors. Make sure you do some research and get the right type for the job you are doing. You can use epoxy to glue existing parts or to make new parts. To make new parts you have to make a mold of the part which can be done with card board and tape. Pour the epoxy into the mold and allow it ample time to cure. Once it has cured then take it out of the mold and use your files, drill and other tools to finish shaping the part exactly as you need it. For bearing surfaces or high wear areas you can put pieces of metal into the mold at the correct places where needed. Fiberglass or other types of fiber can be added to epoxy as a filler to increase the strength. I have also used metal filings as a filler with good results. Make sure that any material you use as a filler is clean and free of oil.

Electrical parts and Electronics

Caution - If you are not knowledgeable about electrical wiring or electronics then get someone who is experienced to do the work for you or to teach you how to do it properly! This is a safety issue and bad electrical wiring can cause fire or injury.

Electrical wiring

You should inspect the electrical wiring on all machines, old or new. The electrical cords that go to the plug and foot pedal are favorites for cats and dogs to chew on. Also cords are damaged by being caught under chair and table legs. Most older machines (vintage machines) have rotted electrical wiring if it has not already been replaced. Rotted wiring has cracks, is gummy, falling apart, dry or otherwise has lost flexibility and become stiff and brittle.

Check all wires inside the machine as well, there are wires on most machines that run from the power cord to the power switch, light, motor and foot pedal.

If you have damaged cords or wires they must be repaired or replaced. Damaged cords and electrical wiring can cause fires or electric shock. If there is damage to the insulation (plastic covering) of the cords but the wires are not damaged you may be able to tape the cords with electrical tape to repair the problem.

Inspection - Feel the cords and wiring for newer lamps and appliances around your house to get an idea of what good wiring should feel like. Now feel and look at the wiring on your sewing machine. If you see bare wire or if the insulation is damaged or going bad then the cords need to be replaced. The same is the case for internal wiring inside the machine, motor, light and foot pedal.

Lights

LED Lights - Some newer machines use LED lights. These lights very rarely go bad, if your machine has LED lights and they don't work then it is probably a power supply issue and beyond the scope of this book, someone with experience troubleshooting electronics could troubleshoot it.

Incandescent Lights - Most older machines and some newer machines use incandescent lights. These are small light bulbs that look similar to a night light bulb. Make sure that you replace the bulb with the correct wattage bulb. If you put in a bulb that is over the specification for your machine then the light will overheat and could melt the wiring or other parts or could be hot enough to burn you. When you remove the old bulb you can usually find the wattage written on the bulb or the base of the bulb. Some machine have the recommended wattage on the name plate of the machine or on a label in the area of the light. Most machines take a 15 watt bulb. There are two types, screw-in base and bayonet style base.

- The screw-in type is just like a miniature normal light bulb and unscrews in the counterclockwise direction. If the bulb does not unscrew and feels stuck then you may have a bayonet type.
- The bayonet type bulb must be pushed in against a spring and then rotated in the counterclockwise direction about 1/8Th turn to remove (after 1/4Th turn it will just pop out). To replace you must align the pins of the base with the slot in the socket and then push the bulb in against the spring, then turn clockwise about 1/8 turn to lock in the bulb. A bayonet type bulb is pictured below, on the right it has been inserted into the socket but has not yet been turned clockwise 1/8Th turn to lock it in.

Foot controllers

Foot controllers for home machines come it two categories, Low Voltage and High Voltage. These kinds are not interchangeable.

Low Voltage - Most electronic sewing machines use low voltage controllers (see the chapter "Sewing Machine Basics" for a description of what an electronic machine is). In general if your machine has a needle up/down button, touch screen or LCD display it is electronic. On most electronic machines the foot controller will unplug from the machine with a small plug that looks similar to a headphone plug for a Walkman or iPod. The low voltage controller in the picture below has this type of plug. In the low voltage controller there is just a simple potentiometer (small electronic part similar to that which is used as volume control on a radio) that is connected by two or three wires. The potentiometer tells the machine how hard you are pressing on the foot pedal and then the machine actually controls the motor using an electronic circuit inside the machine. Only a low voltage is sent to the foot controller. These controllers are light weight and made of plastic. Usually low voltage controllers must be replaced if they become defective, you could try to open it up and see if there are any loose parts, but most of the time it is a broken potentiometer or broken plastic parts and must be replaced. Generally you must use an exact replacement if you replace the potentiometer, substitutions will usually not work.

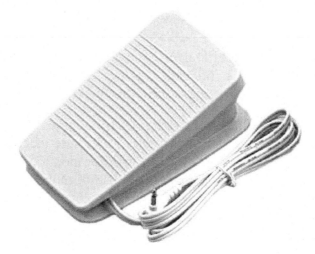

High Voltage - These controllers control the speed of the machine by actually controlling the power that goes to the motor. They run at the full line voltage coming from the wall plug. AC or AC/DC foot controllers come in several types and if you are running your machine from a standard AC wall plug power then any of these types can be used for replacement. The reason that I specified standard AC wall plug power is that the carbon pile type controller will also work with DC power (like from large batteries), but the resistive and solid state types will not.

Carbon pile controllers - These controllers have been used for the last 80 years and are still made today for replacement use. They use use a round stack of carbon pellets to create the resistance to control the motor speed. There is a spring that pushes the carbon pile (pellet stack) together to increase the motor speed when the foot pedal is pushed. This type of controller can be purchased on eBay and at sewing machine supply outlets new for under $20 and is the most popular replacement controller due to the low cost. These controllers can get hot if you are running your machine at low speeds for long periods of time. If you are experienced at repairing electric appliances you may be able to repair and adjust a carbon pile controller, but in general it is best to just replace it with a new one if you are having problems due to the low cost. A typical carbon pile foot controller is pictured below.

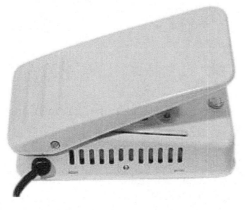

Solid state controllers - This type of controller uses a small part called a TRIAC or SCR to control the power. Solid state controllers generate very little heat and run cool to the touch so they are desirable if you are going to run your machines at low speeds much of the time. Solid state controllers are more expensive then carbon pile controllers and cost $25 or more from eBay and on line parts sellers. When solid state controllers break sometimes they can be repaired if you are skilled in electronics repair and have soldering skills, however it is probably best to just do a replacement. Notice that the solid state controller below has "Electronic" printed on it. This does not mean that it is a low voltage electronic controller as described earlier in this section. This can be confusing. The best way to tell if a controller is a low voltage electronic type is to look at the end of the cord to see what the plug looks like. If the plug looks like a iPod headphone plug then the controller is low voltage electronic, if the plug looks big and heavy duty it is probably the high voltage solid state type.

Electronics

Electronic machines have both mechanical parts and electronic parts. Some of the mechanical parts can be serviced in the same manner as in a mechanical machine. Most electronic machines are difficult to impossible to repair without a service manual.

Servicing the electronic parts in an electronic machines is beyond the scope of this book but in general electronic machines use circuit boards with electronic components mounted on them to control the operation of the machine. Some machines have plugs and connectors on these boards that can be unplugged enabling the board to be removed from the machine. In this case it is possible to substitute the circuit board with another identical board to troubleshoot through the process of elimination. If you have access to parts this can be an effective way to troubleshoot these machines. If you have or are able to get a service manual then the service manual may have diagnostic procedures that can be used to isolate the malfunctioning part or circuit board. Most electronic machines are repaired by replacing the bad circuit board, few circuit boards are actually repaired by replacing a bad component on the board.

If you are skilled in electronics repair then there is nothing particularly difficult or unusual about the electronics that are used in sewing machines and you should be able to dive right in, but a service manual would still be needed for all but the most minor repairs.

Getting Parts

eBay

eBay is a great source of parts for older machines, both home and industrial. There are many sellers on eBay that buy older machines and part them out. Also there are some larger businesses that sell new parts on eBay.

Home machines

For newer home machines you can buy parts directly from the manufacturer in some cases, but in other cases this may not be possible. For example as of the date this book was written Brother will not sell internal parts for newer home machines directly to the general public. They say this policy is to discourage home users from trying to do repairs. They feel that if they sell the part and the repair does not go well, the consumer will blame them. There is some truth to this, the newer mostly plastic machines can be hard to service and adjust without special knowledge and equipment. The problem is that the home user then has to go to a dealer to buy parts, and the dealers sometimes charge very high prices.

If the manufacturer will not sell you the parts and the local dealer is overhanging, you can search the Internet and call one of the larger on-line parts suppliers and usually get a better price. Some of these suppliers are listed in the chapter "Links and Information Sources".

Industrial machines

For industrial machines you can buy parts from the manufacturers or from dealers. Most parts for industrial machines are reasonably priced, I have not run into many dealers that overprice parts or play games. Industrial dealers primarily do business with other companies and are normally very professional. Some industrial manufactures and dealers are listed in the chapter "Links and Information Sources".

Parts machines

Another option is to inexpensively buy a used machine of the same type as your machine and use the machine as a parts machine or "donor machine". In this case you will have a supply of parts to last you quite a while as long as the machine has the parts that you need in good condition.

Used machines can be purchased at very low prices if they are not in good condition. The best sources are Craigslist, garage sales and Goodwill stores. I have purchased many machines for $10 each.

eBay is another option for buying parts machines but the shipping cost can sometimes negate any savings.

Buying & Selling Sergers

Buying new home machines

Amazon.com

For home machines Amazon consistently has good prices and good customer service. However, before you buy you should make sure that the machine is actually sold by Amazon and ships from Amazon. Some items that are listed on Amazon are actually sold by other sellers. If you look, it will clearly say on the product listing page if the item is sold by Amazon or by another "Amazon seller". I am not saying that other sellers are bad, but on these items you need to be aware that Amazon is not the seller so you should do some research and find out about the seller and only buy if you trust the seller. Some sellers are good, some are less reputable.

I use Amazon as a benchmark to check prices for new items. Most of the time it is hard to find a better price. Amazon also has a good return policy if your machine or parts arrive dead, or you don't like the item you ordered. Watch the time that is allowed for returns so that if you are going to return an item you do it in time.

eBay sellers, Amazon sellers and on-line sellers

There are many sellers of new machines that sell through eBay and on-line. Each of these sellers is different. Some are good and others are bad. Do your research and only order from sellers that you trust and feel comfortable dealing with. The landscape of sellers changes all the time so I do not feel comfortable recommending favorites. Sellers that have worked for me in the past may not work so well for you now.

eBay feedback ratings are useful. If an eBay seller has a high positive feedback rating and many sales then they are probably a good seller. Feedback on eBay is done by the seller and not by the item. I have relied upon the eBay feedback system for many high dollar purchases and have had very few problems. I have found the eBay feedback system is more reliable then hours of Internet research of non-eBay sellers. On eBay the items are not guaranteed by eBay and each seller has its own guaranty policy.

The Amazon feedback ratings that you see on most product pages for products sold by Amazon sellers are for the product and are not the cumulative feedback for the seller. If you click on the seller you can pull up a cumulative ratings for the seller. Amazon has what they call an "a-z return guaranty" that covers all sellers sellers. Read about this on Amazon and make up your own mind about if this makes you feel more secure about buying from an Amazon seller.

I have not found a reliable way to get feedback on random on-line sellers that are not on eBay or Amazon. A Google search may or may not turn up any reliable information. Sometimes calling on the phone and talking to them is a good option!

Local stores

I try to buy local if possible, but sadly most local retail stores in my area have high prices and I end up buying on-line most of the time. Sometimes I will buy from the local store anyway just to support them, because it is good to have a local store for convenience sake and I want them to stay in business.

Buying new industrial machines

Industrial sewing machines are sold by industrial sewing machine dealers. They are also sold on eBay and Amazon. Some industrial sewing machine dealers have very good prices, just as good as eBay or Amazon prices. Amazon and eBay have a limited selection of models, going to an industrial sewing machine dealer you will find a much larger selection. Industrial sewing machines are heavy. Buying from a local dealer at a good price may be the best option because you will not have shipping expenses. Check on-line and then call your local dealers to compare prices and service. Local dealers normally service what they sell, this could be a big advantage. Industrial dealers primarily do business with other companies and are normally very professional. Some industrial manufactures and dealers are listed in the chapter "Links and Information Sources".

Buying used machines

Used home machines can be purchased from eBay, Craigslist and some local sewing machine stores. Also resale shops, garage sales and Goodwill stores. Pay attention to shipping cost if you are buying on eBay, used sewing machines are heavy and the shipping costs can add up to more than the cost of the machine!

Most used machines are sold as-is (no guarantee) so plan on having to oil and adjust the machine and allow some extra time and money in your budget for this. A used machine will often need some repairs or parts. If you want a machine that is perfect then get a new machine! Some eBay sellers claim that their used machines are fully serviced and adjusted. Some of these sellers do a good job and the machines are as claimed, other sellers just wipe the machine down with Windex so it looks good in the pictures and have no idea what they are talking about. Look at the feedback ratings and read the actual feedback. Packing is a big issue, you don't want a machine that has been damaged in shipment. Ask the seller about how they pack their machines, if they double box, what kind of packing material is used, etc. Look in the feedback comments to see if other buyers have said anything about the packing, either good or bad. If needed you can offer to send the seller $5 or $10 additional funds for extra packing material and double boxing. Sometimes this is more effective then paying for insurance because you are preventing the damage instead of trying to collect for the damage later which can be a headache and waist of time.

Used industrial machines can also be purchased from eBay and Craigslist. Most industrial sewing machine dealers also sell used machines and sometimes at good prices. Some industrial dealers have huge inventories of used machines. If you buy from an industrial dealer they may guarantee the machine or are able to provide service and adjustments. If you are buying from eBay or any dealer that is out of your local area pay attention to shipping cost.

Selling used machines

For selling used machines under $200 Craigslist is the best way to go. This is because sewing machines are heavy and difficult to pack well. If you sell them on eBay, by the time you add up your time, seller fees, shipping costs and other fees it is not a good deal. Otherwise you may prefer to give less expensive machines that you are not using to your favorite charity! To determine the asking price for machines you are selling you should look at previous sales on both eBay and Craigslist.

Links & Information Sources

The following are various serger & overlock machine related links you may find helpful.

New machines

I buy most of my new home machines from Amazon and have not found another seller that I consistently use. You should check out other sellers and compare for your self though, you may find other sellers that work good for you. Although Amazon does sell Industrial machines I prefer to buy my industrial machines from a local industrial sewing machine dealer to avoid shipping charges and hassle.

amazon.com

The top selling sergers on Amazon

http://www.amazon.com/gp/bestsellers/sergers

Used machines

http://www.ebay.com/

http://www.craigslist.org/about/sites/

Industrial machines & parts

http://www.hendersonsewing.com/

http://www.archsewing.com/index.html

http://www.strima.com/

http://www.sloanmachinery.com/

http://www.miamisewing.com/Page_2x.html

http://www.keysew.com/

Home machine parts

http://www.sewingpartsonline.com/

http://www.sew4less.com/index.php

http://sewcat.com/

http://www.autumnsewing.com/

Servo motors

http://www.reliablecorporation.com/Products/Motors/Sewquiet-5000

http://www.consew.com/List/Machine-Stands/Servo-Motors

http://www.endurosaves.com/

http://www.artisansew.com/motors.html

http://www.advancedsewing.com/servomotorscontrols.html

Home serger manufactures

babylock.com

http://www.brother-usa.com/homesewing/

http://www.elnausa.com/

http://janome.com/

http://www.jukihome.com/

http://www.pfaff.com/

http://www.singerco.com/

http://new.husqvarnaviking.com/

Industrial machine manufacturers

http://www.brother.com/as_oc/ism/index.htm

http://www.feiyue.cn/

http://www.gemsy.com/

http://www.juki.co.jp/index_e.html

http://www.juki.com/jus.html

http://www.merrow.com/

http://www.pegasusofamerica.com/

http://www.reliablecorporation.com/Products/SINGLE-NEEDLE

http://www.rimoldiecf.com/index.php?page=company

http://parts.singerco.com/

http://www.siruba.com/

http://www.yamata.com/index.htm

Theory and Information

http://en.wikipedia.org/wiki/Category:Sewing_machines

http://en.wikipedia.org/wiki/Sewing_machine

http://www.juki.co.jp/industrial_e/customer_e/books_e/index.html

http://www.fashion-incubator.com/

http://www.uspto.gov/web/patents/classification/uspc112/defs112.htm

Manuals

http://www.ismacs.net/free-sewing-machine-manuals-list.html

http://parts.singerco.com/html/inst_manuals.html

http://www.singerco.com/support/replacement-parts-chart

http://parts.singerco.com/IPinstManuals/

http://parts.singerco.com/IPsvcManuals/

http://www.dixiesewingmachine.tzo.com/SERVICE%20MANUAL.htm

http://www.hendersonsewing.com/manual.asp

http://www.sewingmanuals.com/index.htm

http://www.sewusa.com/Sewing_Machine_Instruction_Manuals.htm

http://sewingwishlist.com/janome.html

http://riccar.com/help/manuals/

Needles

http://organ-needles.com/english/

http://www.dotec.com.tw/about.htm

http://www.beisselneedles.com/index.html

http://www.groz-beckert.com/cms/en/

http://www.schmetzneedles.com/

Thread

http://www.amefird.com/

https://www.guetermann.com/shop/en/view/content/

http://www.coatsindustrial.com/en

Glossary

A, B

American & Efird - A large manufacturer of high quality thread. Produces many types of threads including advanced and technical threads.

Amp - Abbreviation for ampere, this is a unit of measurement of electrical current. With home sewing machine motors for example the motor may have a rating of 1 Amp, you will usually see this listed on the identification tag on the side of the motor. This rating is the most current that the motor will use under normal use. Just looking at the Ampere rating by itself is not meaningful, you must also know the voltage. This is also listed on the identification tag. You can then multiply the voltage by the amperage to find the power that the motor will use. The unit of measurement for power is in watts. So, putting this all together; if the motor runs at 120 volts and is rated at 1.4 amps then it will consume 120 x 1.4 = 168 watts. This is the power that the motor can consume at maximum load (like if you are sewing very heavy fabric). To control the speed of the motor the foot controller will reduce the voltage that goes to the motor. If you are going at less than full speed and sewing lighter fabric the motor would consume much less, for example at medium speed the motor may draw .6 amps, because the foot controller would be sending less than 120 volts to the motor (lets say 75 volts for example) so if we do the math we get 75 volts x .6 amps = 45 watts.

Automatic Back Tacking (or automatic tacking) - This is the automatic sewing of reinforcement at the beginning or end of seams to prevent the stitches from pulling out. See Reinforcement.

Automatic Needle Threader - A device to aid in the threading of the sewing machine needle. Most are not completely automatic but only aid in threading the needle, the thread is placed and held over the threader and a lever is pushed to cause the threader to move into place over the needle and make the thread go through the eye of the needle. The threader is then retracted.

Automatic Needle Up/down - This is a function that is available on electronic machines. There is a button that when pressed will cause the needle bar to move the needle to the down position or the up position. In addition most electronic machines can be set to always stop with the needle up or down. For making pivot turns (using the needle as a pivot point) it is handy to set the machine to stop with the needle in the down position. For regular sewing the machine would be set to stop with the needle in the up position.

Automatic Presser Foot Lifter - This function is available on some more expensive home machines and on some industrial machines. The machine will automatically lower the presser foot at the start of the seam and raise the presser foot at the end of the seam. Most machines that have automatic presser foot lift capability can be programmed to raise the presser foot and stop with the needle in the down position for making pivot turns. This function can also be combined with automatic back tacking and/or automatic thread cutting on some machines.

Automatic Reinforcement - See Automatic back tacking.

Automatic Thread Cutter or Thread Trimmer - This function is available on some electronic home machines and on some industrial machines. The thread is cut automatically at the end of the seam, when the machine is stopped or when a button is pushed (depending on the capability of the machine and how the machine is set to operate).

Axial center - The axial center of something is the axis or center of rotation if it were rotated. For example the axial center of a ball would be the very center point. To find the axial center of a cylindrical object like a needle you would rotate the needle like a shaft and the very center point of the rotation (the point that moved the least amount) would be the axial center point.

Balanced Stitch - For most overlock stitches the point that the two looper threads interlock or cross each other is supposed to be at the edge of the fabric, in this case the stitch is said to be balanced. If the crossing point is not at the edge of the fabric then the tensions must be adjusted to move the crossing point to the edge of the fabric.

Bar Tack - A bar tack is a length of closely spaced zigzag stitches (usually about 10mm to 20mm long) that is used to reinforce areas of stress or weakness in garments or sewn products. A bar tack is used to reinforce the openings for pockets on jeans, to attach belt loops and straps, secure the ends of webbing, etc.

Bar Tack Machine - This a special purpose sewing machine that only makes a bar tack.

Basting - Also called tacking, this is a temporary seam used to hold fabric in place until permanent construction seam can be used. The basting stitch is made in such a way that it can easily be removed, with a lockstitch sewing machine this can be accomplished by loosening the needle thread so that the lock will be pulled to the bottom of the fabric. This allows the bottom thread to be pulled out later. This is usually done when assembling a complicated design so that the parts can be roughly tacked together and once they are held in place the permanent stitching can be done without the parts moving around. Sometimes a basting stitch is used for the cuffs of pants because this allows the stitch to easily be removed if the hem needs to be raised of lowered. Industrial basting machines are available that use a single thread chain stitch that can be easily removed (stitch type 101).

Basting Stitch - See Basting.

Bed - This is lower flat or cylindrical part of the sewing machine that the fabric travels across during sewing. Flat bed machines use a flat bed and are used to sew fabric that is laid flat during sewing. Cylinder bed or post bed machines use a smaller cylinder shaped bed that can accommodate sewing tubular shaped fabric such as sleeves, pants legs or shoes.

Belt - see drive belt

Bearing - A bearing is mechanical device used support a part and allow movement of that part such as a shaft that rotates. If the shaft were just bolted to the machine it could not move or rotate. Instead a bearing is attached to the machine and then the shaft is inserted into the bearing allowing it to rotate in a precise position. In a sewing machine most bearings are rotational but some are sliding such as the needle bar and presser bar. There are many types of bearings such as the sleeve bearing, ball bearing, roller bearing and cone bearing. Most bearings use some form of lubricant (oil or grease). The lubricant goes in between the metal or plastic surfaces of the bearing to prevent the surfaces from actually touching. In this way wear of the load bearing surfaces of the bearing is reduced. There are open bearings and sealed bearings. Open bearings are open to the air. Sealed bearings have a seal that is usually made of rubber to close the bearing from the open air and to contain the lubricant. This greatly prolongs the life of the lubricant but makes it more difficult to add lubricant later.

Bearing Play - This is how tightly the bearing constrains the supported part. In the case of a shaft you can grab the shaft and try to move it to feel the play (such as the shaft of a motor). There are two types of play in a shaft bearing, axial play and radial play. Some bearings (such as cone bearings) have an adjustable amount of play. Most bearings are not adjustable, if the bearing has too much play it must be replaced.

Bearing Surface - See bearing.

Bight - The width of a zigzag stitch.

Blind Hem - A hem made with a blind stitch so that the stitching is not visible from the outside of the garment. Blind hems are also used in draperies.

Blind Stitch - The blind stitch is used to do hemming of pants and dresses and is used because it is less visible then regular types of stitches. There are several variations of the blind stitch depending on what kind of machine is used to make it. 1. If made by a zigzag machine then this it is a variation of the zigzag stitch in which a straight stitch is made for several stitches and then a single zigzag stitch is made followed by several more straight stitches and so on. 2. If made by a blind stitch machine it is a modified zigzag stitch made using a curved needle that only penetrates the back of the fabric leaving no visible stitches on the front of the fabric. 3. If made by hand it is similar to #2.

Box Feed - A type of feed dog driving mechanism in which the feed dogs move in a rectangular motion as opposed to a elliptical motion on a typical machine. This results in better controlled movement of the fabric and less chance that the fabric will move while the needle is in the fabric which could cause the needle to bend.

Brother - A large Japanese based manufacturer of home and industrial sewing machines.

Brushes - A part of a universal or DC motor that is used in most home sewing machines. The brushes are small parts that conduct electricity from the power wires to the commutator of the motor as the motor rotates. The brushes slide on the surface of the commutator. Brushes have a long service life but after many hours they need to be replaced or the motor will loose power and finally stop running. Some motors have 2 small caps on the outside of the motor that can be unscrewed to access the brushes for easy replacement. Other motors require disassembly for brush replacement. The brushes are made of carbon and graphite. Also see Commutator and Universal Motor.

C, D

Cast Iron Body - Older home and industrial machines use cast iron metal for the body and bed of the machine. Cast iron is strong and rigid and the machines made of this metal are robust and have a long service life. However it is a very heavy material and has been replaced with aluminum (which is much lighter) in modern machines.

Chain - This is the looped threads made by a chain stitch sewing machine or serger when the machine is run without fabric. It looks like braided strands of thread. Unlike a lockstitch sewing machine that should not be run without fabric, a chain stitch machine can be run with no fabric and will produce a chain.

Chaining Off, Chained Off - After a chain stitch machine or serger is threaded it can be run for a short time to produce some chain and verify that it has been threaded and set up correctly. This is known as chaining off and once this has been done you can say that the machine has been chained off.

Chainstitch - A type of stitch formed with a needle and one or more loopers. In a chain stitch the thread is looped to interlock and forms a chain. Unlike a lockstitch a bobbin is not needed, so a chainstitch machine can sew for a long duration without having to stop and change or reload bobbins.

China Feiyue - A large Chinese manufacturer of home and industrial sewing machines. In the USA and some other countries they are sold under the Yamata brand name (owned by China Feiyue). They also make machines for many other brand names. Some industrial sewing machine dealers refer to China Feiyue machines as "Family Machines" because of the large number of brands they are sold under.

Clearance - The distance between two parts such as the hook and the needle in a sewing machine. Clearance is measured with a feeler gage or a micrometer.

Clutch Motor - A type of motor used to power industrial sewing machines. Clutch motors are always turning when they are turned on and a clutch is used to connect the motor to the sewing machine and to control the speed of the sewing machine. Clutch motors typically rotate at 1725 RPM (lower speed) or 3450 RPM (higher speed). RPM stands for rotations per minute.

Coats & Clark - A manufacturer of thread based in the UK.

Computer Interface - A connection to a computer. Some electronic sewing machines or embroidery machines have a USB or Ethernet connection to connect the built in computer to an external computer such as a laptop or personal computer. This is used for transferring patterns or stitches to the machines computer.

Computer Numeric Control - See CNC

Cone Bearing - A type of bearing used in many home and older industrial sewing machines. The bearing consists of a metal cone that fits into a cup to form the bearing surface.

CNC - Computer control of a machine such as a sewing machine or embroidery machine. CNC stands for Computer Numeric Control. Using a small computer built into the machine the machine is able to do complex work such as sew complicated stitches or embroidery patterns.

Commercial - In sewing commercial means the same thing as professional or small business. A commercial application could be a dry cleaner, Taylor shop, etc.

Commutator - Part of a Universal motor. The commutator is a ring of contacts (part of the rotor) that conducts power from the brushes to the rotor.

Construction Seam - A seam that is used to assemble an item or for structural applications, in other words where stress could be applied to the seam during use. This is contrasted to a decorative seam that probably will not come under stress.

Construction Stitch - A stitch that is suitable for use in a construction seam.

Coverstitch - A stitch made with 2 or 3 needles and needle threads making parallel rows and one or two loopers and looper threads crossing back and forth similar to a rounded zigzag. This stitch is used in garment construction and is called a cover stitch because the crossing looper threads can provide a cover to hide the joining of two pieces of fabric.

Cross Thread - If a screw is improperly inserted into a threaded hole or nut and tightened the threads will not align correctly and the threads of the screw will try to cut into the threads of the hole or nut. This will damage both.

Cursor Controls - Buttons on a sewing machine that control the position of the cursor on an LCD display.

Cutting Table - A table used for cutting fabric. If the table is to be used with a hand powered rotary cutter a cutting mat will be needed to cover the top of the table to prevent damage.

Cutter - The blades of a serger that trims the seam allowance of the fabric as it runs through the machine.

Cylinder Bed - A cylinder bed sewing machine has a round tubular shaped bed (the area around the feed dogs and hook). A cylinder bed sewing machine is used to sew sleeves, pants legs, shoes and other items that would be difficult or impossible to sew on a flat bed sewing machine. In home machines this is called a free arm and is made with a removable flat bed so that the machine can be used as a cylinder bed or flat bed machine.

Decorative Stitch - Any of many types of stitches used to primarily to decorate. Most decorative stitches are variations of the lockstitch but chain stitches can also be used for decoration such as in jeans using thick thread.

Default Settings (electronic machines) - Default settings are the settings that the machine powers on with or returns to after a reset. For example if the stitch width is set to 3mm and the needle position is set to the center, the machine may fall back to the default setting of 5mm stitch width and left needle position when it is restarted. Some machines will remember the last used setting when turned on and off, in this case the machine can said to power on "last set" instead of "with default settings".

Default Tension Setting - The recommended tension setting for general purpose thread (or in the case of heavy duty machines whatever thread the machine was designed for). The default tension setting may be indicated on the tension knob if it is numbered or could be stated in the owners manual. This should be the starting tension you use when you first start using the machine and is the setting that the machine was set up with at the factory.

Denim - A heavy twill fabric made of cotton used for jeans and outer wear.

Differential Feed - A type of feed used on most sergers and some industrial machines. Two separate feed dogs are used, one in front of the needle and one behind the needle. These feed dogs can be set to run at different speeds. If the front dogs are running faster than the rear dogs the fabric will bunch. If the front dogs are running slower than the rear dogs the fabric will stretch. In this way the feed can be tweaked for any type of fabric including difficult stretch fabrics that would be very hard to sew normally.

Direct Drive - A sewing machine motor that directly drives the main shaft of the machine with no belts or clutches. Direct drive is becoming popular in newer industrial sewing machines and overlock machines.

Drive Belt - A belt that is made of rubber and fiber strands used to transfer power from the motor to the main shaft of a sewing machine. Drive belts come in many types including V-belt, cogged belt, notched belt, rubber round belt and leather belt.

Drive Belt Tension - The tightness of a drive belt in relation to the motor pulley and handwheel pulley. If the belt is too loose it will slip. If the belt is too tight it will cause accelerated wear.

Drive Belt Tension Adjustment - The adjustment to loosen or tighten drive belt tension, this is normally done by screws that allow the movement of the motor bracket on the frame of the machine.

Drop Feed - A type of feed (means of moving the fabric through the machine) in which feed dogs move below the fabric and contact the fabric with sharp teeth to grab the fabric and pull it through the machine. This is the most common type of feed and is used in most sergers and overlock machines. A presser foot is used on top of the fabric to hold the fabric in contact with the teeth of the feed dog. The feed dog moves cyclical motion from front to back and then lowers out of contact with the fabric so that it can reset to the front position before raising into contact with the fabric for the next cycle.

Donor Machine - A sewing machine that is used to supply parts to other sewing machines for repair. A donor machine is usually an older machine that is purchased inexpensively but sometimes new machines are used as donor machines in cases where parts are needed and the parts cost would be more than the cost of another new machine.

Edging Stitch - Any stitch used for terminating the edge of fabrics. The most popular stitch for edging is the overlock stitch but the overlock stitch can not be made by a regular sewing machine (only a serger or an overlock machine) so there are also several overedge stitches that can be used. The overedge stitches are variations of zigzag stitches and can be made by a lockstitch sewing machine.

Edge Finishing - Applying an overlock stitch or overedge stitch to terminate (sew over to prevent fray) the edge of fabrics.

Edge Guide - A metal or plastic guide that can be attached to the bed (or sometimes the foot) of a sewing machine or serger to guide the fabric through the machine a precise distance from the needle.

Electronic - A device (sewing machine in this case) that uses electronic parts and circuits inside. Electronic circuits include parts such as computer chips, transistors, circuit boards, LCD displays, etc. Electronics enable the machine to have advanced features such as automatic thread cutters, automatic needle positioning, automatic needle up/down, automatic back tacking, fancy decorative stitch patterns, combinations of stitches, mirror imaging of stitches, monogramming, etc.

Electronic Machine - A serger or sewing machine that uses electronics (see above). This is in contrast to a "mechanical" machine that does not use electronics.

Electronic Control - Control of sewing machine parts by electronic circuits and sensors. Some parts that could be electronically controlled include the motor, presser foot, needle bar position, thread cutter, etc.

Electric - Simple types of electric devices such as universal motors, mechanical power switches, older control pedals, light bulbs, power plugs, wire and power cords. These devices have all been around for over 100 years and do not incorporate newer "electronic" parts such as transistors, computer chips, sensors, LCD displays, etc.

Electric Motor - A basic motor of the universal, split pole or capacitor start types. Electric motors have been made for over 100 years. This is in contrast to an electronic or servo motor that has built in control circuits that use transistors and computer chips.

Electronic Motor - See servo motor.

Electrical Wiring - Copper wire used to connect electric parts in a sewing machine such as the power cord, motor, light and power switch. Electrical wire has a plastic or cloth covering (insulation) to prevent it from making contact with the frame of the machine or with other wires or parts.

English System - see Imperial System.

Eye - An opening in a sewing machine needle just above the tip and below the scarf that the thread goes through.

Fabric Guide - See edge guide.

Feed Dogs - Moving metal parts with teeth used to pull fabric through a sewing machine. The feed dogs are mounted below the needle plate and their movement is controlled by a mechanism that causes them rise into contact with the fabric, move the fabric, lower out of contact with the fabric and then move to the forward position to start another cycle before rising again.

Feed Dog Height - The amount the feed dog teeth protrude through the needle plate when the feed dogs are in the up position. On some machines this can be controlled with a feed dog height control for best operation with thick and thin fabrics.

Feed Dog Height Control - See feed dog height.

Feed Dog Height Adjustment - See feed dog height.

Feed Dog Timing - When the feed dogs move in relation to when the needle bar moves. On a drop feed machine the feed dogs should only move the fabric when the needle is in the up position and is completely out of the fabric. Most machines allow this to be adjusted using set screws under the machine, but this will rarely need adjustment unless the machine is damaged or has a traumatic event.

Feed Type - The type of feed setup that a machine has to move the fabric through the machine. The most common is drop feed and other common types are needle feed, compound feed, walking foot and tractor feed.

Feet - Plural of foot.

Flat Bed - The bed of a sewing machine is the area of the machine where the needle plate and feed dogs are located and the fabric passes over during sewing. In a flat bed machine this area is flat and broad allowing the fabric to be easily fed and controlled by the operator. Other types of beds are cylinder bed, post bed and free arms, these beds are used to sew odd shaped items with limited clearance such as sleeves.

Flywheel Effect - Also known as rotational inertia. As a sewing machine starts and builds up speed the weight of its moving parts need to be accelerated. The heavier the moving parts are the longer this will take. Also the heavier the parts are the longer the machine will take to slow down. As the needle moves down and pierces the fabric the machine will try to stop, but the momentum of the moving parts will help keep the machine moving as the needle pierces through the fabric. Putting this all together we find that a machine with heavy moving parts is slower to start and stop but is able to keep going as the needle is able to pierce through thick fabric. A machine with lightweight moving parts is fast to start and stop but lacks the ability to pierce through thick fabric as well. So the design engineers settle on a compromise between speed of starting and stopping and what is called piercing power. The weight of the moving parts are largely controlled by the weight of the handwheel, it is used as a flywheel and the thickness and type of metal determines the weight and inertia. Other factors that effect starting, stopping and piercing power are the size and type of the motor and if the motor is servo controlled (electronically controlled)

Foot - The part of a sewing machine that holds the fabric in contact with the feed dogs to allow the fabric to move through the machine. There are many types of feet available for most machines.

Foot, Snap-On - A type of foot used in home sewing machines that snaps into a foot holder shank that mounts on the the presser bar of the sewing machine. Once the foot holder shank is mounted on the presser bar any snap-in foot can be snapped in or removed from the machine in seconds with no tools. Most modern home machines come with snap-in type feet.

Foot Controller - See foot pedal controller.

Foot Pedal Controller - A foot pedal with internal electric or electronic parts that is used to control the power output of a sewing machine motor. The foot pedal is connected to the motor with electrical wires. The motor gets no power when the pedal is not depressed. As your foot applies pressure and moves the pedal downwards electric power is made available to the motor. When the pedal is completely depressed the motor is at maximum power.

Forced Oil Lubrication System - This is the type of lubrication system used in most industrial sewing machines that is similar to the lubrication system used in automobile engines. An oil pump is used and oil is pumped from a reservoir in the bottom of the machine through tubing to all of the critical bearings. After oil exits the bearings it drops down to the oil reservoir to be used again. The oil reservoir is similar to an oil pan in a car engine. Most machines have an oil filter and dip stick of sight glass to check the oil level.

Free Arm - See cylinder bed.

G, H, I, J, K

Gage - A measurement device of some type. In sewing machine adjustment and maintenance some of the gages used are the micrometer, scale, calipers, etc.

Gauge - see gage.

Gear Drive - The use of metal or plastic gears to interconnect or drive the motor or bottom and top shafts of sewing machines. Other means of driving these parts are belt drive or lever drive. Gear drive is characterized as being very reliable if metal gears are used, however plastic gears have a history of reliability problems due to aging and disintegration or cracking of the plastic over time.

Gutermann - A German manufacturer of thread.

Hand Stitching Needle - A type of sewing needle made for hand sewing, the eye is located on the opposite end of the needle from the tip.

Handwheel - A flywheel and pulley mounted to the main shaft of a sewing machine with a smooth exposed outer surface to allow the rotation of the machine by hand when needed. Most machines have handwheels that rotate in the counterclockwise direction. The handwheel is used to slowly advance the machine for delicate stitching or to manually position the needle to the up or down position as needed. Also see Flywheel Effect.

Harp Space - The harp space of a sewing machine is the space between the needle and the body of the machine that is open for fabric to move during sewing. Most home machines have about 6-1/2 inches of harp space and most industrial machines have 9-/12 inches or more.

Head - The main frame and body of a sewing machine. This may or may not include the motor. Most modern home machines have the motor built in to the head of the machine and the head is the whole machine. Some older home machines are Treadle powered machines and the head is mounted to a table and is driven by a belt from the Treadle mounted in the bottom of the table. Most industrial machines have the head mounted in a heavy table and the motor is mounted below the table, the machine is driven by belt connecting the handwheel to the motor pulley.

Heavy Duty - For home machines a heavy duty machine is slightly heavier and more robustly constructed than a regular machine and can sew through somewhat thicker fabric or a few more layers of fabric. For industrial machines a heavy duty machine would be a very strong and tough machine with reinforced parts that can be used to sew leather, canvas, boat sails and other thick materials or many layers.

Hemming Machine - A specialized machine designed to a hemming stitch or blind stitch. These machines can not be used for general purpose sewing.

Imperial System - The Imperial System and the US Customary Measurement System are measurement systems consisting of inches, feet and yards used in the UK and USA. Most vintage sewing machines made in the UK and USA use parts that are dimensioned in these systems. Modern machines are all made using dimensions from the ISO Metric System. This is important to know because parts such as screws, nuts, shafts and bearings are not compatible between the two systems and can cause confusion if the user is not aware of this. A part can look like a perfect replacement yet not fit correctly because the systems are slightly different.

Industrial Sewing Machine - Industrial machines are designed for heavy use in manufacturing (factories). Sometimes they are also used in small business (commercial use) and by home sewers when extra durability or high speed is needed. Most industrial machines have forced oil lubrication systems and other features to allow for continuous used with decreased maintenance requirements.

ISO 4915 - The ISO standard for stitch and seam specifications. It was adopted form the US military Federal Standard 751a. When you see a stitch called out with a number in a sewing machine manual, product design specification or pattern for a sewn product or garment it is referring to ISO 4915 or Federal Standard 751a. Some examples are the lockstitch type 301 or the chainstitch type 301.

ISO - Stands for International Standards Organization. This is the international organization that sets standards for many specifications for business, manufacturing, industry, computer technology and other industries.

ISO Class System - See stitch specification system.

ISO Stitch Class Number - See stitch specification system.

Janome - A large Japanese manufacturer of sewing machines, sergers and embroidery machines. Janome makes primarily home machines. Also see the chapter Sewing Machine History.

Juki - A large Japanese manufacturer of sewing machines that makes many models of Industrial sewing machines and overlock machines. Also see the chapter Sewing Machine History.

Knee Lifter - A lever operated by the users knee to raise the presser foot of a sewing machine. Most industrial machines have knee lifters. Some high end or heavy duty home machines have them.

Knife - see cutter.

L, M, N

Land - A slight bulge in a sewing machine needle between the eye and scarf. Some chain stitch needles have a second land between the scarf and the long groove to aid in the formation of the loop in machines that do not have needle bar rise.

LCD - Liquid Crystal Display. This is a type of display used in modern sewing machines and embroidery machines.

LED Light - Light Emitting Diode. A type of light that used very low power and has very long life. It is used for lighting and as indicator lights in sewing machines and other electronics.

Lock Point - The place where the upper and lower threads cross. If the tension is adjusted correctly the lockpoint will be in the center of the fabric.

Lockstitch - This is the stitch made by a general purpose sewing machine. It is a symmetrical type of stitch (the same on the top and bottom of the fabric). The lockstitch is made with a needle thread (needle thread) and a bottom thread (bobbin thread) that cross in the center of the fabric. The lockstitch is the most widely used stitch type for sewing machines and all home sewing machines and many industrial machines use the lockstitch.

Lock up - If a sewing machine is frozen and the handwheel cannot be turned it is said to be locked up. See the chapter Maintenance under the sections Restoring Old Machines and Bearings.

Looper - A moving part of a sewing machine or serger used to make a chain stitch or overlock stitch. The looper has a tip and an eye for thread like a needle and mounts on a shaft that is controlled by a drive mechanism in the machine. Some machines have more than one looper.The tip of the looper moves past the scarf of the needle (or 2nd looper on machines with more than one looper) and catches the thread in a similar manner to the hook in a lockstitch machine.

Looper Clearance - The distance between the tip of the looper and the scarf of the needle or 2nd looper. This is a critical adjustment and must be set properly for the machine to function.

Looper Timing - The tip of the looper must cross the center of the scarf of the needle (or the scarf of the 2nd looper in machines with two loopers) as the machine rotates. The tip must not cross the scarf too late or too early. This adjustment is known as looper timing.

Loupe - An optical magnifier used to look at small objects such as needle points. A photographic loupe is configured to set on a table and look at flat objects, a jewelers loupe is made to be attached to eye glasses or held next to your eye and look at all types of small objects such as watches, jewelry and sewing machine parts.

Lower Thread Path - The path of the bobbin thread in a lockstitch sewing machine or looper thread in a chainstitch machine or serger. This includes all guides, bobbin cases and tension assemblies.

Maximum Speed - The maximum speed that a sewing machine is rated to handle. This is usually given in SPM (stitches per minute). With home machines this is the maximum speed the machine will go with the built in motor. With industrial machines where the motors and machines can be purchased separately this is the maximum speed that the machine should be run at. The motor and pulley ratios should be selected to never exceed this speed or damage to the machine could occur.

Mechanical - Something that is physical as opposed to electronic. Gears, shafts and levers are all mechanical.

Mechanical Machine - A type of sewing machine that does not have electronics. All old vintage sewing machines are mechanical machines.

Machine Head - See Head.

Memory - The ability and locations to save and recall settings on an electronic sewing machine. Memory is also used to store stitch patterns and embroidery designs.

Memory Recall - See above.

Metric System - The ISO (international) measurement system used on all modern sewing machines. Some vintage machines use the Imperial System. This is important to know because parts such as screws, nuts, shafts and bearings are not compatible between the two systems and can cause confusion if the user is not aware of this. A part can look like a perfect replacement yet not fit correctly because the systems are slightly different.

Micrometer - A device for accurately measuring small parts and objects. Mechanical micrometers are made in both metric and imperial systems. Electronic micrometers are usually switchable to work with either system.

Mock Overlock Stitch - Same as overedge stitch. See overedge stitch.

Mock Safety Stitch - A stitch made by a two needle four thread serger or overlock machine that looks similar to a five thread safety stitch.

Motor - In the case of sewing machines all motors are electric motors. An electric motor converts electric power into a rotary mechanical motion of the output shaft. See Electric Motor. For home machines see Universal Motor. For industrial machines see Clutch Motor or Servo Motor.

Needle - See sewing machine needle.

Needle Bar - The needle bar in a sewing machine is a cylindrical metal part that is about the size of a pencil (or slightly smaller). The needle mounts to the needle bar with a needle clamp. The needle clamp holds the shank of the needle firmly to the needle bar. The needle bar is driven up and down by a linkage from the main shaft as the machine sews. The needle penetrates the fabric on the lower portion of its stroke. The needle bar is mounted in bearings that allow it to slide up and down easily as the machine operates.

Needle Bar Height- The needle bar on a sewing machine must be adjusted so that the tip of the hook is about in the center of the scarf of the needle (or slightly lower) when the needle is in the down position. This adjustment is known as needle bar height. The adjustment is made on most machines by loosening a set screw that clamps the needle bar driver to the needle bar and then moving the needle bar up or down to the correct position, then the set screw is tightened. Unless the machine experiences a traumatic event such as the needle hitting the needle plate this adjustment will not need to be made often or at all.

Needle Bar Rise - The distance the needle rises from lowest position before the tip of the hook approaches the center of the scarf. It is necessary to have needle bar rise to form a loop that can be caught by the point of the hook.

Needle Clamp - See needle bar.

Needle Deflection - As a sewing machine needle contacts and then penetrates the fabric during operation of the machine the needle will flex. This flex is known as needle deflection. A small amount of flex (under .25 mm) is normal and not a cause for concern but if there is a large amount of flex (more than .5mm) the needle can collide with parts of the machine such as the needle plate of hook. This collision will cause the needle to permanently bend or break and could cause damage to the machine. Heavy fabrics require a larger needle size to minimize needle deflection, the larger needle diameter will make the needle stronger and stiffer. Excessive needle deflection and breakage can result from improper operation of the machine such as the operator pushing or pulling the fabric instead of letting the feed dogs do the work of moving the fabric though the machine.

Needle Hole - The small hole in the needle plate of a sewing machine that the needle goes through as it travels to its lowest position.

Needle Plate - The needle plate is a metal plate that covers the feed dogs and parts of the drive mechanism in the bed of a sewing machine. The needle plate has slots for the feed dogs to protrude through and a hole for the needle to go through. The needle plate attaches to the bed of the machine with screws or some sort of clamping parts and may be removed for cleaning and inspection of the feed dogs or to aid in visibility during lubrication and adjustment of the machine.

Needle Shank - The top part of a sewing machine needle that is inserted into the needle clamp to hold the needle to the needle bar.

Needle Size - The size of the needle is determined by the diameter of the blade measured just above the scarf.

Needle System - Sewing machines needles have three major parameters, size, system and type. The term "Needle system" means "needle specification name". The needle specification includes such things as the length of the needle, the diameter of the shank, the distance from the butt to the eye, etc. Every needle manufacturer makes up a system of numbers to identify the needles that they make. Sometimes these numbers make sense and have a logical basis, but some manufacturers have numbers that are arbitrary and make no sense at all. In all cases these numbers (or "needle system") will identify the product and can be thought of as a product name. Make sure that you always purchase the needles of the "needle system" that are recommended by the manufacturer of your sewing machine, needles from different needle systems are usually not interchangeable.

Needle Thread - Also called upper thread, the needle thread is the thread that goes through the needle of a sewing machine.

Needle Threader - See automatic needle threader

Needle Type - Sewing machines needles have three major parameters, size, system and type. The type of a needle usually describes the tip and eye but may also pertain to other parts of the needle. Needles come in many types including sharp point, ball point, denim, twin, quilting, etc.

Needle Up/down Button - A button on an electronic sewing machine used to move the button to the up or down position.

Needle Up/down Control - A setting on an electronic sewing machine used to set the operation of the machine so that when the machine is stopped the needle will stop on the up position (normal) or the down position (for doing pivot turns). On some machines the needle up/down setting functionality is incorporated into the needle up/down button and there is not a separate control or menu setting.

O, P, Q, R

Oil - See Sewing Machine Oil.

Oil Wick - Some sewing machines have an oil hole that leads to a small oil pan. There is are one or more cotton ropes that leads from the oil pan to the bearings that require lubrication. The oil will saturate the cotton rope and follow the rope from the oil pan to the bearings. This is known as wicking action and the rope is therefore called an oil wick. The whole system is known as an oil wick type lubrication system.

Overcasting - See Edging Stitch.

Overlock Machine - A specialized type of machine that makes the overlock stitch. The overlock stitch is used for edge finishing and seaming. Overlock machines can only sew on the edge of the fabric. An overlock machine is similar to a serger. Technically speaking, sergers have a built in cutter to trim the edge of the fabric and overlock machines do not have a cutter, but in common usage the term "serger" and "overlock machine" are interchangeable and mean the same thing. Sergers and overlock machines come in both home and industrial versions. For more on sergers and overlock machines check out our companion book "The Serger & Overlock Master Guide".

Overlock Stitch - An overlock stitch is a multi-thread chain stitch in which at least one thread passes over the edge of the fabric. Overlock stitches are can be used for edge finishing or to join two pieces of fabric together and finish the edge in one operation. An overlock stitch can not be made by a lockstitch or general purpose sewing machine.

Owners Manual - A manual that is written by the manufacturer of a sewing machine for that specific model of machine. The owners manual will have exact information and instructions for a specific machine such as threading diagrams, lubrication requirements, tension adjustment procedures, etc.

Parts Manual - A manual that is written by the manufacturer of a sewing machine for that specific model of machine. The parts manual will list all parts used in the machine along with the part numbers. Most parts manuals also include detailed drawings and diagrams showing the location of the parts in the machine and what the parts look like.

Pfaff - A German manufacturer of sewing machines, sergers and embroidery machines.

Piercing power - The downward force that a sewing machine can apply to the needle bar to drive the needle through the fabric. Also see Flywheel Effect.

Premium Sewing Machine Brand - Some brands of expensive home sewing machines are positioned in the market as premium brands. Premium brands sell lower quantities of machines at a higher profit. These machines usually have many features.

Presser Foot - The presser foot is the part of the sewing machine that presses down on the fabric from above and forces the fabric into contact with the feed dogs that are mounted in the bed of the machine below the needle plate. The sewing machine foot attaches to the shank and the shank attaches to the presser bar of the machine. Some feet are permanently attached to the shank while other feet use a snap-on style shank and are able to be removed from the shank. Also see Snap-On Foot.

Presser Foot Awareness - This is a feature of some electronic sewing machines. When a stitch is selected the machine will tell you (through the LCD screen) what foot to use for that particular stitch.

Presser Foot Lever - This is the hand lever mounted close to the presser bar that is used to raise and lower the presser foot. Some machines have both a knee lifter and a presser foot lever.

Presser Foot Lift - This is the clearance measurement between the bottom of the presser foot and the needle plate of a sewing machine when the presser foot is in the up position. Sometimes there are two levels that the foot can be raised to, the normal level and a high clearance level that can be achieved by further movement of the presser foot lever. On some machines that have knee lifters a higher level can only be achieved with the knee lifter and not the hand lever.

Presser Foot Pressure - The force that the presser foot presses down with when in the down (sewing) position. This force is adjustable on some machines by presser foot pressure control.

Puller Feed - This is a type of feed that is used in some industrial sewing machines and overlock machines that incorporates a feed wheel or tire set that is behind the needle and normal feed dogs. These additional wheels or tires are driven by shafts and belts. The fabric is pulled by the wheels in addition to the feed dogs and this allows trouble free feeding of very thick or unmanageable materials but limits the machines ability to sew around tight curves.

Pulley - A special grooved wheel that is mounted to the output shaft of a motor or other rotating shaft. A belt is used between two pulleys to transfer rotational power from the driving pulley to the receiving pulley.

Reinforcement (at the beginning and end of seams) - Reinforcement is done at the beginning and end of seams by sewing about 1/2 inch (12mm) in the opposite direction (by putting the machine in reverse). This is done to prevent the stitches from pulling out at the beginning and end of the seam. Some sewing machines can do this automatically, they have a special button or can be programmed to do this at the start and end of every seam. In this case it is called automatic back tacking or automatic tacking.

Reliable - A manufacturer of industrial sewing machines based in Canada.

Rotary Cutter - A cutting tool for cutting fabric that uses a sharpened metal disk (similar to a pizza cutter) for a blade. There are hand powered rotary cutters and electric rotary cutters. Hand powered rotary cutters need to be used with a cutting mat. Electric rotary cutters have a built in sliding base that rolls over the table surface and can cut on any flat surface because the blade never actually comes in contact with the table.

RPM - Revolutions Per Minute. This is a measurement of the speed of rotation of a motor, shaft or wheel.

S, T

Scarf - The scarf of a needle is the smooth flattened area of the shaft just above the eye of the needle. The scarf is flattened to allow the hook to pass between the shaft and the thread and make it easier for the hook to catch the thread.

Seam Failure - This is the coming apart of a seam because of thread breakage, fabric ripping or other failure mode. See the chapter Stitches under the section Seam Failure Causes.

Seam Elasticity - The ability of a seam to stretch without failing when put under stress.

Serger - See Overlock Machine. Also check out our companion book "The Serger & Overlock Master Guide".

Serger Thread - General purpose serger thread is usually T27 and can be 2 or 3 ply. This is sold as serger thread in retail sewing stores.

Service Life - The expected life of a machine or part in hours or years.

Service Manual - An adjustment and repair manual that is written by the manufacturer of a sewing machine for that specific model of machine.

Servo Motor - Servo motors have a built in computer that monitors and controls the motor. Because a computer is controlling the motor a clutch is not needed. Servo motors are lighter in weight than clutch motors for the same power output. Servo motors have adjustable top speeds and can be set to run in forward or reverse rotation.

Sewing Machine Needle - A sewing machine needle is a needle that is specifically designed for use in sewing machines and has the eye close to the point and a shank for attaching it to a sewing machine. The sewing machine needle also has a scarf to allow more clearance for the hook or looper as it passes by the needle.

Sewing Machine Oil - For sewing machines a clear or white "spindle oil" is used. This type of oil stains fabric as little as possible and has very low friction properties to reduce wear on the machine.

Sewn off - After a sewing machine is threaded it can be tested for a short time on a piece of scrap fabric to verify that it has been threaded correctly and functions correctly. This is known as sewing off and once this has been done you can say that the machine has been sewn off.

Shank (foot) - The part of a sewing machine foot that mounts to the presser bar of the machine. There are several types of shanks and they are not interchangeable. For home machines there are high shanks, low shanks, slant shanks and some manufactures use non-standard shanks. For industrial machines there are high shanks, Consew style walking foot shanks and several non-standard shanks.

Shank (needle) - See Needle Shank.

Singer - A US manufacturer of sewing machines. Also see the chapter Sewing Machine History.

Speed Range Control - This is a control on electronic machines that sets the top speed that the machine will run. On some home machines this control can also be used to control the operating speed of the machine if the foot pedal is not plugged in to the machine so that the machine can be operated with no foot pedal.

Split Phase Motor or Capacitor Start Motor - This is the type of electric motor used in clutch motors that are used with industrial sewing machines. These motors run smoothly and have a long service live but are not power efficient.

Spool Pin - A metal or plastic pin mounted to a sewing machine or thread stand to hold a spool of thread during sewing and prevent it from moving.

Stabilizer - A paper of synthetic material that is layered with fabric during sewing or embroidery to stop the fabric from stretching or otherwise moving while the machine is running. The stabilizer also helps the fabric to feed through the machine. The most stabilizer materials are designed to tear away after sewing.

Stepper Motor - A type of motor used for control applications in an electronic sewing machine. For example a stepper motor could be used to control the needle bar position or the feed dog height.

Stitch - Interlocking, braided or chained threads used to attach, bind or decorate fabric or other material.

Stitch Counter - A stitch counter is a measuring tool that is used to measure a portion of a seam and determine how many stitches per inch or stitches per millimeter there are.

Stitch Length - The distance between stitches in a seam. Measured by counting the number of stitches per inch (SPI) or measuring the length of each stitch in millimeters. Newer machines use millimeters and some older machines use SPI. To convert stitch length in millimeters to SPI the equation is 25.4/mm=SPI. In this equation 25.4 is the number of millimeters in one inch. For example if you wanted to convert a 2mm stitch length to SPI then the equation would be 25.4/2=12.7 so your answer is 12.7 SPI.

Stitch Length Control - The length of each stitch the machine makes is controlled by the stitch length control.

Stitch Specification System - The US military set up a standard specification system for seam construction and stitch types that is still widely used today in the garment and sewn products industries. The latest version of this specification is Federal Standard 751a. The specification has also been adopted by the International Organization for Standardization as ISO standard 4915. The standardized stitch types let you know exactly what stitch to use when you have a pattern or sewing instructions that call for a stitch number (such as a 301 lockstitch or 504 overlock). Stitch specification numbers are also used in some sewing machine specifications sheets and instruction manuals to identify stitches.

Stitch Width - The width of a stitch.

Stitch Width Control or Dial - A control on a machine used to set the stitch width.

Stitches Per Inch (SPI) - A unit of measurement used to specify stitch length. SPI is not very intuitive for some people, because the higher the number of stitches per inch the shorter the stitch length. Also see Stitch Length.

Stitches Per Minute (SPM) - The speed of a sewing machine, the number of stitches the machine can sew in one minute.

Straight Stitch - A lockstitch or chainstitch in which the needle advances from stitch to stitch in a straight line to form a seam. This is in contrast to a zigzag stitch in which the needle moves from side to side.

Structural Stitch - A stitch that is used to assemble an item or for structural applications, in other words where stress could be applied to the seam during use. This is contrasted to a decorative stitch that probably will not come under stress.

Systematic Troubleshooting - A troubleshooting technique whereby a complex system (such as a sewing machine) is divided up into parts or subsystems and each part or subsystem is scrutinized in some sort of order or progression. For example if a machine appears frozen then the power system can be checked starting at the power cord and wall plug a through the power switch and finally the motor. Next the mechanical systems could be checked starting with the motor shaft rotation, drive belt, handwheel, main shaft rotation, etc. See the chapter Troubleshooting.

Take-up Lever - The take-up lever is a lever in a sewing machine that removes the loop from the needle thread and tightens the stitch after the needle raises from the fabric.

Tension - For the sewing machine to function and the stitches to be well formed the thread must be controlled and under the correct amount of tension or drag. Tension is a resistance or drag applied to the thread so that the thread will not freely unroll from the thread spool in an uncontrolled manner during sewing, leading to tangled thread and poor stitching.

Tension Adjustment Knob - A knob on a sewing machine used to control the tension of the needle thread (and looper threads in a chain stitch machine). Some machines have numbered tension adjustment knobs so that it is easy to remember an exact setting and return to that setting at a later date.

Tension Disks - To provide tension a sewing machine has adjustable friction disks or friction parts in the thread path and bobbin case. These friction disks or friction parts are pushed together by a spring and pinch or squeeze the thread to create tension.

Tension Release Mechanism - Most sewing machines have a device that releases the needle thread tension disks when the presser foot is raised. This is done so that the needle thread can be pulled from the needle at the end of the seam allowing the fabric to be removed from the machine.

Tex System - The Tex system is the most widely used thread size measurement system and is used worldwide. It is the ISO standard (International Organization for Standardization). The Tex size is determined by the weight (in grams) for 1000 meters of thread. The Tex system is called a fixed length system because a fixed length of thread (1000 meters) is weighed to determine the thread size. The Tex system is intuitive because the numbers increase as the thread sizes get larger.

Timing - See Looper Timing.

Timing Belt (Cogged Belt, Crimped Belt) - A belt with teeth or ridges running crosswise to the direction of travel on the contact surface of the belt. A timing belt is used with cogged pulleys that have similar teeth on the contact surface. This creates a similar drive setup to a chain and sprockets in which no slippage is possible.

Thread Failure - Thread used in a seam or stitching breaking, rotting or become frayed.

Thread Guide - Any wire loop or other device on a sewing machine used for the purpose of controlling thread or routing thread along the thread path on its way through the machine

Thread Path - The path that thread takes when going though a threaded machine. The proper thread is given in the threading diagram for the machine or in the owners manual for the machine.

Thread Ply - A number of strands are twisted together to form most thread. These strands are also known as a ply, fold or yarn. For example a Three-ply thread is made from three strands or plies that have been twisted together.

Thread Ripper - A hand tool for removing seams from fabric.

Thread Stand - The purpose of a thread stand is to hold thread cones or thread spools in a vertical position and allow the thread to be fed to a sewing machine with little or no resistance or pulling. A thread stand consists of a base and a tree, the base holds one or more spools or cones of thread. The tree mounts to the base and extends over the thread. The top part of the tree has thread guides.

Thread Tails - Hanging threads are left attached to the end of a seam when fabric is removed from a sewing machine after sewing. These threads are known as thread tales and can be cut off or possibly sewn into another seam if you are continuing to sew in the same area.

Thread Twist - When thread is manufactured it is twisted to add strength and so that the strands will stay together. Most sewing machines are designed for thread with a left hand twist (Z twist) and most common thread is left hand twist. Thread with a right twist is known as "S twist". Thread of the correct twist must be used in sewing machines or the thread will snarl and knot while feeding through the machine.

Thread Size - There are many thread size systems and most of them are different and the sizes are not compatible between systems. The most popular thread size system is the TEX system. See the chapter Thread for more information on the many thread size systems.

Threading Diagram - A diagram that shows how to thread a sewing machine and the proper thread path of the machine. The threading diagram is part of the owners manual for the machine but may also be printed on the machine or the case of the machine. Most sergers have a threading diagram on the inside of the lower looper cover.

Thumb Screw - A machine screw with a large head that is designed to be turned by the fingers and thumb instead of requiring a screw driver. Thumb screws are used on most vintage sewing machines to attach the pressure foot.

Torque - The turning force on a shaft such as a the output shaft from an electric motor. Some of the units of measurement for torque are inch-pounds, foot-pounds, newton-millimeters and newton-meters. For example 10 inch-pounds of torque would equal the turning force of one pound that is applied to a 10 inch lever attached to a rotating shaft. To put this to a practical application lets say that you had a nut that is supposed to be tightened to 5 inch-pounds of torque. In this case if you turn the nut with a wrench (which is a lever) and grab the wrench exactly 5 inches from the center of the nut and apply 1 pound of force to the wrench you will have tightened the nut to exactly 5 inch-pounds of torque.

Traumatic Event - A traumatic event for a sewing machine is any event that is intense enough to cause the machine to come out of adjustment or cause the breakage or bending of parts. Some examples of traumatic events are needle collisions, dropping of the machine, jamming of the hook, freezing due to insufficient lubrication, etc. Needle collisions occur when the needle deflects (bends) and collides with the needle plate causing the machine to stop rotation in an abrupt and violent manner.

U, V, W, X, Y, Z

Universal Motor - This is the type of motor used in all home sewing machines made before 1980 and many newer machines. The universal motor is called "universal" because it can run on both AC power or DC power. The universal motor is relatively small for the power output and is quite reliable and easy to manufacture. Universal motors use electric coils (wire) for both the armature (also called the rotor, the part that turns) and the stator (the stationary part of the motor). No permanent magnets are used. There is a commutator and brushes to conduct power from the body of the motor to the turning rotor. See Commutator, Brushes, Electric Motor.

V-Belt - A drive belt with tapered sides to match the tapered grove in a pulley. V-belts are used on most home sewing machines built before 1990 and most industrial sewing machines that are not direct drive. Also see Belt.

Variable Speed Controller - See Foot Controller.

Viking - A Swedish manufacturer of home sewing machines, embroidery machines and sergers. Also see the chapter Sewing Machine History.

Voltage - A unit of measurement of electricity. In the USA and some other countries 120V is used in homes. In Europe and many parts of Asia 240V is used. A sewing machine, electric light or any other type of equipment must be rated for (designed for) the correct voltage that is locally available, a 120V device can not be used with 240V electricity or damage and fire will result. The required voltage for most devices are listed on a label on the bottom or side of the device, sometimes close to the power cord. There are step down transformers and converters available to convert from 120V to 240V and visa verse.

White - A US manufacturer of sewing machines.

Zigzag - The zigzag stitch is a lockstitch formed when the machine moves the needle from side to side evenly on every stitch (ISO stitch type 304).

Zigzag Width - The width of a zigzag stitch.

Made in the USA
Monee, IL
19 May 2020